Desires in Conflict

"From his many years of experience counseling homosexuals struggling to find FREEDOM and WHOLENESS, Joe Dallas has written a very PRACTICAL and HELPFUL book. It will bring much needed ENCOURAGEMENT to those who DESIRE CHANGE and much needed instruction to those of us who counsel them in the process."

—David A. Seamands,
Professor of Pastoral Ministry,
Asbury Theological Seminary

"INVALUABLE to Christian people who struggle with homosexuality, as well as to their families and friends. Filled with INSIGHT and PRACTICAL suggestions. *Desires in Conflict* provides a very balanced approach to the subject. I'm very pleased to give it an A+!"

—Barbara Johnson, author of
Where Does a Mother Go to Resign?
Founder of Spatula Ministries

"At last—a book WRITTEN DIRECTLY TO THE CHRISTIAN man or woman with homosexual desires. Most books talk *about* the struggle, not *to* the struggler. If you want ANSWERS for your own life, this may be the MOST IMPORTANT book you will ever read.

—Bob Davies,
Executive Director,
Exodus International

"The Church has few advocates for the development of a Christlike character. There's a plethora of quick-fix options. But Joe Dallas' book offers a WORKABLE approach to sexual and emotional sanctification ILLUMINATING the power of GOD'S GRACE at work in the sincerely repentant soul. *Desires in Conflict* will help EQUIP the Church to deal with this delicate issue. Celebration is forthcoming when the homosexual struggler finds an impassioned ally in the Church, and the Kingdom receives back its members."

—Raymond Jones,
Licensed Marriage, Family, and Child Counselor,
Certified Addictions Specialist

Desires in Conflict

JOE DALLAS

HARVEST HOUSE PUBLISHERS
Eugene, Oregon 97402

Resources

Educational materials by Joe Dallas on homosexuality and related issues are available through Genesis Counseling. For a free catalogue of the Genesis Audio and Video Cassette Series, and for more information on seminars by Joe Dallas, please contact:

Genesis Counseling
177 North Glassell
Orange, CA 92680
(714) 502-1463

DESIRES IN CONFLICT

Copyright © 1991 by Harvest House Publishers
Eugene, Oregon 97402

Library of Congress Cataloging-in-Publication Data

Dallas, Joe, 1954-
    Desires in conflict / Joe Dallas.
    Includes bibliographical references.
    ISBN 0-89081-897-5
    1. Homosexuality—Religious aspects—Christianity
    2. Gays—Pastoral counseling of.   I. Title
    BR115.H6D35   1991
    261.8′35766—dc20   91-10270
                                                 CIP

Printed in the United States of America.

98 99 00 01 02 03 /BC/ 10 9 8 7 6

Contents

Part Five: The Struggle for Identity

Part Six: The Other Struggle

Introduction

The problem of homosexuality among Christians is one of the church's best-kept secrets. Though most believers agree with the cliche "Christians aren't perfect; just forgiven," there is often an additional (though unspoken) agreement that our imperfections go only so far. We admit that we sin, but only in "respectable" ways: an occasional lie, a touch of greed—nothing drastic. Seldom do we recognize sexual problems in the church, though we'll occasionally admit that a Christian might battle with lust. Rarely if ever do we consider that the object of his or her lust might be someone of the same sex.

Yet the church is composed of people from all backgrounds, bringing with them any number of spiritual, psychological, and sexual problems, homosexuality included.[1] Ideally these problems would vanish after conversion to Christ; in reality, they often remain, challenging both the church and the struggling believer. The believer is challenged to overcome his struggles through ongoing sanctification and discipline, while the church is challenged—no, *mandated*—to offer support and encouragement to the struggler. Both parties need to recognize the issue if it is to be dealt with effectively.

But nobody's talking. The church doesn't seem to think it has any homosexual members, so these people, in turn, find scant encouragement in the church. Theirs is a problem which isn't supposed to exist among Christians, so they struggle alone, silently praying for deliverance and aching for the comfort of a listening ear or a bit of compassion. "The time has come," Peter warns in his epistle, "for judgment to begin at the house of God" (1 Peter 4:17). If we are to entertain any hope of addressing the problem of homosexuality in our culture, we'd best begin by addressing it among ourselves.

Desires in Conflict was written with this goal in mind. It is intended to give some reassurance and practical advice to the Christian dealing with same-sex attractions, while offering insight to pastors, family members, and Christians in general, all of whom are or will be directly affected by this issue.

If any issue demands more insight, it's this one. The debate over homosexuality and Christianity is hot, gut-wrenching, and controversial, dividing whole denominations and pitting political forces against one another in the public arena. And, as the song says, "we've only just begun."

This book is an expansion of a series of talks I gave in 1989 to a small group of Christians, most of them homosexually oriented and hungry to resolve their conflict. Rather than just preach on the evils of sexual perversion, I found it effective to outline a process of growth I had seen my counselees go through as they dealt with sexual and emotional problems. I'd recently begun training for the California Marriage Family and Child Counselor's License (as of this writing, I am completing the hours of clinical supervision necessary for state licensing) and much of my work had been done with men and women who were conservative Christians, sexually attracted to their own gender, and very dissatisfied with their homosexuality. They felt, among other things, alienated from fellow believers and convinced that theirs was a unique struggle indicating some major defect in them. "Wouldn't it be better," I thought, "if homosexually inclined Christians could at least know they weren't alone? And wouldn't it help to know what others in their position had gone through when they successfully dealt with homosexuality?" As I reviewed my client's files and noticed similarities in their backgrounds and growth patterns, some important ideas emerged.

The first idea had to do with process versus transformation. Homosexuality doesn't just vanish when a person decides he or she doesn't want it. None of my counselees were insincere or undecided on that point: They no more wanted to be gay than they wanted a third eyeball. They were willing to do anything to be free. The answer in all cases has been to go through a process of growth rather than to expect a quick change. And there's the rub—"process" is a word foreign to the vocabulary of modern Americans.

We are, as Andy Comiskey says, "the people of the immediate."[2] The microwave has usurped the stove, automated tellers keep us out of the bank lines, and liposuction is so much snappier than dieting. Convenience is everything. We resent waiting; if we can't have it now, we figure it isn't worth the trouble.

When a person wants deliverance from homosexuality, this mentality can be lethal. It's led many a person to try shock treatment, exorcism, and sexual experimentation with the opposite sex in hope of a quick cure. The result is always the same: failure and disillusionment.

That's because homosexuality (including lesbianism) is not one isolated problem. (That is the second idea, one which puts the subject in better perspective.) It is symptomatic of other problems that are deeply ingrained and often hard to detect. Like the red light on a dashboard, it indicates that something under the hood needs to be checked.

Scripture bears this out. In the first chapter of Romans, Paul describes homosexual passions as a result of something deeper:

> Although they knew God, they did not glorify Him as God, nor were thankful, but . . . their foolish hearts were darkened. . . . For this reason God gave them up unto vile passions. For even their women exchanged the natural use for what is against nature. Likewise also the men, leaving the natural use of the woman, burned in their lust for one another (Romans 1:21,26,27).

Aside from condemning homosexual lust, Paul is pointing out its symptomatic nature. The real problem cited here is universal sin, of which homosexuality is but a symptom. This holds true psychologically as well as theologically. The homosexual orientation is caused by other factors, and they, not just the sexual attractions, need to be dealt with.

The third idea, which will be repeated throughout this book, has to do with the complexity of the subject. There are few things we can say about homosexuality that will always hold true. On the authority of the Bible, of course, we can unhesitantly state that homosexuality is unnatural and contrary to God's intention for sexual experience, and that homosexual acts are always, without exception, immoral. Beyond

9

these points our generalizations will be faulty. There is no such thing as a "typical" homosexual. There is no one reason people become homosexual. And there is no one method of dealing with homosexuality which will be effective for all people. An intelligent discussion on the subject must include a respect for the complexity of homosexuality in particular and human sexuality in general. It remains a mystery in many ways, and there is much we still don't know about it.

I've also seen how poorly this issue has been handled by the church and the mental health industry. My clients have, in the past, usually received pretty bad treatment from both.

Since I work primarily with Christians, I've heard plenty of stories about their past attempts to deal with homosexuality through spiritual means. Those attempts included a visit to their pastor or Christian counselor. More often than not, the advice they were given ranged from the simplistic to the bizarre: "You need a deliverance"; "You're probably not really saved if you have those feelings"; "Try fasting."

Of course these devices failed, leading these people to try secular therapy. There they were advised to simply accept their sexual feelings and not resist them. The real problem, they were told, was not their homosexuality but society's homophobia. This left these people in a frustrating spot: the church had few answers for their sexual problems, and secular professionals were telling them they had no problems!

This book takes a different approach, one which I hope will help people by taking the uniqueness of the individual into consideration while pointing out what others have experienced, what issues they dealt with, and what worked most effectively in their cases.

So let me emphasize from the outset that I don't pretend to know a universal "cure" for homosexuality. Nobody does. Instead, I've taken the experiences of men and women who have counseled with me over a period of time and compared their experiences with some prevailing theories about homosexuality. You may see some or much of yourself in their stories, and gain fresh insights into yourself and your situation.

Additionally, I've tried to prioritize the growth process

(sanctification, if you will) which is the common experience of all Christians. That's why Chapters 1 through 3 place emphasis on obedience and integrity, while most of the remaining chapters are more conceptual. No changes can occur, no growth can be attained, unless the foundation of integrity is laid through repentance, discipline, and commitment. This is true in all of life; doubly so when dealing with sexuality.

Chapters 5 and 6 are the most theoretical portions of the book. When borrowing from the ideas of others I've tried to give them full credit; likewise, when presenting my opinion I've tried to clarify that it is just that—an opinion. Opinions are useful, of course, but just as the Bereans in the book of Acts searched the Scriptures to see if the things that Paul was preaching were true, you need to check the theories in *Desires in Conflict* for yourself.

Although no one book can provide all the answers for a person needing to know how to deal with homosexuality, I do think it is useful to know what methods have worked for others. In Chapters 7 through 12, I've outlined the specific struggles and challenges I've seen the majority of my counselees face: the maintenance of sexual integrity, the courage to confront relationships and patterns that are unhealthy, the search for the "perfect parent," the establishment of healthy and nonsexual friendships, and the problems of childhood trauma, emotional dependency, and gender identity. Not all readers will relate to all these struggles, but I believe many or most readers will relate to most of them.

You may ask why faith in Christ isn't enough to correct the problem. Are we not, having been born again, new creatures seated in heavenly places? Are not all things made new, as Paul said? And isn't God sufficient to deliver us from any problems we have, homosexuality included?

Yes to all of the above. But God has created us with emotional needs that, by His design, can only be satisfied through people. It was He, after all, who looked upon Adam and said, "It is not good for man to be alone." Adam already had God; God declared that he needed more. I will argue throughout this book that homosexuality is a relational problem having its roots in some relational deficit between parent and child,

11

or child and other children, or other people and himself. Since it is a problem generated by faulty relations, it finds its resolution through healthy relationships. Salvation, which secures our eternal relationship with God, is only the beginning of emotional health. When we, as a result of our salvation and the benefits that come with it, begin to experience human intimacy as He intended us to, then we find healing for damaged emotions, faulty self-perceptions, and unsatisfied longings. It's not that faith in Christ isn't enough; instead, faith in Christ is the beginning.

My editors have wisely advised me to write *Desires in Conflict* conversationally, as though it were one long counseling session rather than a textbook. I've followed their advice by writing in the first person—me to you—which may sound presumptuous, but actually makes it easier to communicate. Besides, if you are the one to whom this book is addressed, you've probably heard and read many things *about* you. Perhaps you'll appreciate a work that is written *to* you.

Now you can't discuss homosexuality without running into problems of semantics. The choice of terms available is bewildering. Should one refer to homosexuals as "gays"? Should the practice of homosexuality be referred to as "the gay lifestyle"? And how should you—a Christian who has homosexual attractions but doesn't want them—be referred to? A recovering homosexual? An ex-gay? A straight wanna-be?

As I'll point out later in this book, I prefer not to call anyone "a homosexual" because I feel the term is too limiting and not entirely accurate. And "gay" is out, as far as I'm concerned, because it's too vague. To some people it means homosexual while to others it is a more political, social term not limited to but including a homosexual orientation. And I can't keep referring to you as "a Christian who has unwanted homosexual attractions." So for the sake of brevity and only within the confines of this book, I'd like to refer to you as a Fighter. You are one, you know. You're fighting an internal battle with desires you didn't ask for and are most likely trying to resist. You're fighting against the misunderstanding that so many people have about those in your position. You're fighting the urge to throw up your hands in despair, to give up, to give in.

You're fighting to survive, and you're fighting to win. For these reasons, I hope the term "Fighter" will be acceptable to you.

The absence of any reference to AIDS and the presence of Chapters 10 and 11 by Dr. Carol Ahrens deserve some explanation. AIDS is a subject so often associated with homosexuality that it is conspicuous by its absence in this book. But because *Desires in Conflict* is primarily about the emotional process that a Fighter goes through, I couldn't give AIDS anything close to the attention it deserves. For that you'll have to look elsewhere. Let me suggest *The AIDS Epidemic: Balancing Compassion and Justice,* by Glenn G. Wood, M.D., and John E. Dietrich, M.D. (Multnomah, 1990). It's the best resource on AIDS I know of.

As for Dr. Ahrens' contributions on lesbianism and related women's issues, I felt it would be helpful to hear from a therapist who has done extensive work with women. The principles in this book apply to both sexes, of course, but most of my work has been done with men. In some cases there are special problems that are unique to each sex. Promiscuity, for example, is a problem I've found more common among men than women. Likewise, codependency is something I feel (and have been repeatedly told by women) is a more common female issue. I'll leave it for others to decide if the reasons for these differences are cultural, biological, or both.

Carol Ahrens has worked for years with women dealing with lesbianism. She is well-qualified to speak to the special needs these women have, and to offer them sound counsel. Additionally, she has been my clinical supervisor since 1988, and it's to her that I've looked for personal and professional guidance. So I'm sure her contributions will prove to be invaluable to female readers.

I'm deeply indebted to Editors Bill Jensen and Eileen Mason of Harvest House Publishers for their encouragement and belief in this project; to Bill I am especially grateful for a longstanding friendship and for prodding me along to complete this book.

Psychologist Mark Baker has profoundly affected the way I

view sexuality, relationships, and the function of intimacy. His influence can be felt throughout this book. Because he's been a mentor to me, I hope he is pleased.

Dr. Raymond Jones has contributed much-needed criticism, especially of my ideas in Chapter 6. I thank him for his input, which I have taken to heart.

Dr. Carol Ahrens, of course, has been a port in all storms throughout this writing. She has contributed much more than two chapters. Thank you, dear friend.

Special thanks and respect to the men and women who have allowed me, through counseling, to be a part of their journey. They have once and forever changed my life.

To my beautiful Renata Marie.
Thanks, Honey.

PART ONE

The Struggle
for More

1

You Are Here

*Then said Evangelist, "If this be thy condition, why
standest thou still?"*
He answered, "Because I know not whither to go."

—John Bunyan
Pilgrims Progress

Your first trip to a new shopping mall will probably include a stop at the main directory. It's
centrally displayed on each floor, giving an overview of
the mall complex, with each business location named
and categorized. Visual creatures that we are, we like
overviews because they simplify things, framing them
with clear boundaries and definitions. So you appreciate
the directory. It makes the mall seem less intimidating,
more accessible. The directory's reference point is, of
course, the spot marked X saying "You Are Here." It
gives an immediate sense of location. It also indicates
the location of your *goal* in relation to your *current
position*, while giving a clue as to how long it will take
you to get there. The X also lends an air of friendly
support to a bewildered shopper. *(See? You're not lost.
Here's where you are and that's where you're headed.)*
As a Christian struggling against homosexuality—

a Fighter—you could probably use some of that encouragement. Chances are, you've been applying Herculean effort to the struggle, reaping a mixture of success and setbacks. The best intentions seem to be no match for same-sex attractions, and when you begin addressing all the conflicts that go along with homosexuality, you open up a container that makes Pandora's box look like a box of chocolates!

The resulting confusion is understandable. After all, if your only opponent were a single issue (lust, temper, etc.) the fight would be simpler. But this battle is waged against a unique combination of desires in conflict: the desire to love God obediently versus the desire to be loved in a way that God prohibits, the desire for a normal sex life versus the desire to satisfy feelings that seem normal but aren't, the desire to be honest about your feelings versus the desire to be safe from retaliation. It's not just a sexual sin you're fighting, but a deeply ingrained way of responding which seems immune to good intentions. In fact, you may be finding that the more effort you apply to the fight, the harder it is to believe you'll ever win. "The good that I will to do I do not do," laments the apostle Paul, "but the evil I will not to do, that I practice" (Romans 7:19). Sound familiar?

Effort is commendable, but when dealing with homosexuality, effort without strategy is like shadowboxing: Your opponent keeps showing up in different places. Good help in developing such strategy, though, is scarce. That's because in spite of the volumes written about homosexuality, not to mention the controversies now raging over its political and social impact, little guidance has been offered to people in your position. There have been some fine books written for the homosexual wanting to change, but they are sparse and relatively unknown to the general market, eclipsed by the more popular and ever-simplistic "If you're gay, accept it" versus the "If you're gay, you're damned" materials, both of which exclude you. You don't accept "gay" as a desirable state, but you also don't need to be told that homosexual acts are abnormal or biblically condemned. Hearing that is about as useful to you as a sign on the shopping mall directory saying "You Are Lost." With so few resources available to you, it's no wonder you may feel aimless and defeated. A sense of bearing is called for—an understanding of where you are in relation to your goal, what it is you're dealing with, and what you can expect along the way.

You and Others Are Here

Lost shoppers tend to feel alone in their confusion. They assume the people strolling past them know just where they're going and how to get there. This only frustrates them more, making them feel alone and a little stupid, so of course they're relieved when they come across another shopper at the directory looking as lost as they are. At least they're not the only ones in that position!

When counseling Fighters I'm reminded of a similar but more painful position: social isolation. It's one thing to struggle but another thing to feel you're the only one struggling. Worse yet is the fear that if your problem were to be found out, the grace that is normally shown to people with "normal" problems wouldn't be extended to you. Time and again counselees report fear of exposure as being their worst nightmare. Many of them are not sexually active and are committing no moral sin; they just know they're attracted to their own sex. The thought that someone else might detect those attractions frightens them into silence and often avoidance of close relationships. Close relationships, after all, include the sharing of personal problems, and here's one problem that no one seems anxious to discuss.

And time and again, whether through a support group or therapy, these counselees are relieved to learn they're not alone. Or freakish. Or whatever. It feels good knowing that you're not the only one with a problem, not because you necessarily want other people to have problems like yours, but because you want to feel that somebody else understands.

We'll begin, then, by addressing that sense of isolation experienced by others in your position. The "You Are Here" sign for such people should be subtitled "It's Crowded Here." After all, since the Christian church is comprised of people from all parts of society, you can expect its members to represent a variety of problems common to their culture. So with today's large divorce rate, for example, one would expect many divorcees and single parents to be part of the church body. Likewise, alcoholism and drug addiction are commonplace, so the church includes many believers grappling with the effects of substance abuse.

Considering the fact that homosexuality is evident in all aspects of American life, we shouldn't be surprised at the number of Christians who deal with it as well. What *is* surprising is the lack of assistance available to such Christians, in spite of the growth experienced by the few ministries that do offer it.

Exodus International is a good example. Established in 1976, Exodus is a coalition of Christian organizations providing education and support for men and women wanting to grow beyond homosexuality. There are other such coalitions, as well as numerous independent groups doing similar work.[1] And the need for such work is illustrated by Exodus' expansion. A handful of groups made up the network at its inception. As of this writing, Exodus is comprised of 70 ministries across North America. If need begets growth, then Exodus' growth these past 15 years is further proof that there are many people with needs similar to yours.

But if that's the case, why the silence? Why do so many Christian strugglers feel they're the only ones on the planet dealing with same-sex attractions?

Lack of adequate information within the church is usually the culprit, and I believe that this lack of information exists because we've been threatened by any understanding of homosexuality beyond a few select Bible verses.

Of course, the Christian develops his worldview and understanding of humanity from the Bible. That's as it should be. Scripture provides the standard by which we test all theory (2 Timothy 3:16) and on which we base our belief system. Sometimes, though, our understanding of an issue is limited because of our unwillingness to consider theories that are not spelled out in the Bible but which are by no means unbiblical.

Lack of adequate information among Christians regarding homosexuality is a case in point. While there are clear biblical injunctions against homosexual *acts,* there is scant reference in the Bible to the *homosexual orientation*—i.e., sexual *attraction* to members of one's own sex as opposed to sexual *activity* with the same sex. Psychological studies provide some understanding of the homosexual orientation, but many of us are understandably leery of all things psychological. (Considering the anti-Christian bias of so many mental health practitioners, psychology's acceptance among Christians is sometimes astounding!) Nonetheless, ignorance of that secular research which *is* valid has left many Christians unaware of the complexities of homosexuality in particular and sexuality in general. Most Christians, for example, view a homosexual only as a person who commits homosexual acts. The question of orientation is rarely considered. And so the thought that a Christian might have homosexual desires is foreign to most of us. It's usually viewed as a problem "out there" which no true believer could have. But of course many true believers *do* have it. Yet considering the church's lack of understanding, who's going to be brave enough to identify himself as someone having a conflict that isn't supposed to exist among Christians? (When is the last time you heard a person in a public prayer meeting request intercession for his homosexual temptations?)

Lack of adequate information doesn't account for all on the silence of the struggler's part, but it probably accounts for most of it, leaving thousands of Christians sitting in our pews having the same conflicts and bearing the same weight of secrecy. At any rate, the fact remains that you *do* have brothers and sisters with struggles similar to yours, and while it is true that you and your circumstances are unique in many ways, it's also true that your position as a struggler is not rare. You are here, but you are far from alone.

You Are Making Decisions Here

When you confront your status as a Christian with homosexual tendencies, you have to also confront your options, be they right or wrong. No one is forcing you to change. You don't *have* to go straight, nor do you *have* to deny your sexual longings. You have choices, and making a clear analysis of those choices *now* will alleviate a good deal of indecision once you've started your course, because it's going to be difficult for you no matter which course you choose.

Don't misunderstand: I endorse only one choice— full repentance of all homosexual activity and an earnest seeking for sexual wholeness—because that is the only choice that has sound scriptural backing. It's also the only alternative which will be explored and commended in this book. But if you make this choice without recognizing the others, experience has shown that you'll eventually be challenged to determine whether or not it was the right one. If you haven't considered the other options, weighed them, *and consciously rejected them*, you may be setting yourself up for confusion and wavering somewhere down the line. So you may as well determine it now. Recognizing the alternatives to a plan of action doesn't negate your commitment to that plan, but it does settle in your mind what it is you've decided to do and why, and what it is you've decided *not* to do and why. "How long will you falter between two opinions?" Elijah demanded. "If the Lord is God, follow Him; but if Baal, then follow him" (1 Kings 18:21). The prophet was appealing not only to the people's spiritual commitment but to their common sense, assuming that before deciding whether to serve God or Baal they would consider the merits of both. We'll consider your other options in that same spirit.

In essence, you may decide to repent of all homosexual activity and seek sexual wholeness, or you can decide on one of three other courses of action:

1. Maintain the status quo
2. Abandon the faith
3. Compromise scriptural standards

Maintaining the Status Quo

To be undecided is to decide. The decision *not* to make a decision is a decision in itself. Inaction, then, or maintaining the status quo, is a plan of action.

When questioning a counselee about his current situation, I'm interested in knowing what impact homosexuality is having on his life, and how it is being expressed. Are his sexual attractions predominantly homosexual? Are his attractions expressed inwardly (sexual dreams and fantasies), or is he acting them out with other people? If he is sexually active, is his activity limited to anonymous encounters, long-term relationships, or brief affairs? Questions of this type help define the status quo and the consequences of ignoring it.

If your struggle is strictly inward, limited to attractions, fantasies, and the like, you may opt to do nothing about it and find life bearable, if not entirely fulfilling. There are, after all, no outward consequences to deal with, since your issue is between you and God, distinguishing it from sexual activity involving another person. The sin issue is not so apparent here, as the Bible explicitly condemns homosexual *lust and behavior* rather than homosexual *orientation*. Christ's prohibition against lust (Matthew 5:28) certainly applies to the entertaining of sexual fantasies and erotic desires outside of marriage, but not to the unaroused condition of homosexuality. (Or the unaroused condition of heterosexuality, for that matter. A heterosexual male is attracted to women, but he is not always lusting after them. A homosexual male is attracted to men, but he's not always lusting after them.)

So if to you "status quo" means repeatedly confessing to God your episodes of lust and resisting erotic temptations, you could go the rest of your life maintaining it. No one will know unless you want them to; it's your secret.

But is it worth keeping? Remember the high cost of secrecy: *isolation* and the resulting avoidance of whatever help may be available. Isolation, whether it is the isolation of a person or the isolation of a personal issue, is never healthy. Like expanding leaven, it infects and affects the entire personality. So when James admonished us, "Confess your trespasses to one another, and pray for one another, that you may be healed" (James 5:16), he was prescribing an act of spiritual and therapeutic value.

Consider Holocaust survivor Corrie ten Boom, bestselling author, subject of the book and film *The Hiding Place*, and clearly one of the most remarkable Christian leaders of the century. During her imprisonment in the Ravensbruck concentration camp (her "crime" was protecting Jewish Hollanders from the Nazis) she noticed a gradual hardening of her heart toward fellow inmates. She became protective of what few possessions she had and developed a withdrawn, self-centered attitude. It's almost laughable to think that, in the midst of Hitler's death camp, she was concerned about her "attitude." And yet she recalls that her private conflict began to affect her energy and her zeal, both of which were crucial to her survival:

> The special temptation of concentration-camp life—the temptation to think only of oneself, took a thousand cunning forms. I knew this was self-centered, and even if it wasn't right, it wasn't so very wrong, was it? Not wrong like sadism and murder and the other monstrous evils we saw every day.
>
> Was it coincidence that joy and power drained from my ministry? My prayers took on a mechanical ring. Bible study reading was dull and lifeless, so I struggled on with worship and teaching that had ceased to be real. Until one afternoon when the truth blazed like sunlight in the shadows. And so I told the group of women around me the truth about myself— my self-centeredness, my stinginess, my lack of love.
>
> That night real joy returned to my worship.[2]

Disclosure was a release for Corrie, the benefit of which is attested to in numerous Christian and secular studies. Especially revealing is the connection Dr. John White makes between self disclosure and sexual healing. Speaking to the Christian beset with homosexual longings, he says:

> You are not despicable. You were made in the image of God. That image in you may have

been defaced, yet it is still there. And a defaced masterpiece is better far than the unspoiled statue of a third-rate artist. But you will never feel this way about yourself until you take the risk of exposing your inner self—of revealing what you are ashamed of—to someone else. What you need is to warm your soul in the sunshine of another person's respect and understanding and in so doing begin to rediscover respect for yourself. If your problem is not too deeply ingrained, this of itself may be enough to begin to set you free.[3]

So James' advice to disclose our faults one to another has been reaffirmed by modern-day saints and theorists. Disclosure opens the door to intimate communication and support from the people we choose to admit our weaknesses to, and so begins the flow of emotional healing.

So we can assume that, if your struggle is exclusively inward, you can maintain the status quo and reap the benefit of private safety. The consequence of that decision is isolation, anxiety, and the probability that nothing will change.

If you are sexually active outside of marriage, then your struggle is not just between you and God. One or several other people are directly involved, and by allowing the situation to continue you are maintaining a deadly status quo with far-reaching, possibly irreversible consequences. Your decision at this point—whether or not to take action—will shape the direction and the definition of the remainder of your life. (For clarification's sake I will define "sexually active outside of marriage" to mean engaging in any form of sexual activity with another person outside of heterosexual marriage.)

You may be feeling that the payoff for sexual activity outweighs the consequences. But if you think ahead, as any wise person building his life must do, you will realize that while the payoff is temporary, the consequences are eternal. Although the sin itself can be forgiven, its effects may continue their destructive course indefinitely. The "televangelists" scandals of the late 1980's underscore this point. Who would have guessed that ministers of international stature were involved in sexual activities which the average Christian wouldn't even consider? All the more disconcerting is the fact that their ministries continued to flourish long before their private sins were exposed. Regarding sexual sin, two points stand out:

First, it won't just "go away." It requires the light of confession and accountability if it is to be overcome. Secrecy was a common element in those recent scandals. That's usually the case. Sin confessed is sin forgiven, but sin covered up becomes a throbbing, festering entity of its own, exacting a high price of guilt and the fear of being caught. It is exhausting to keep hiding something, but if you're unwilling to bring it to light, hiding is your only other option. Eventually, though, the problem will become too big and too complicated to hide any longer.

Second, and perhaps more important, secret, repetitive sin becomes a taskmaster rather than a pleasure. You may have comforted yourself so far with the notion that you're "getting away with it." But count on it—as long as anything in your life continues to be uncontrollable, you are in bondage to it. For now, the bondage itself is its own consequence. And so to maintain the status quo means not only to remain sexually active, but also to remain under the control of secretive behavior that you neither want nor believe in. If you doubt the need to take action by allowing a fellow believer to walk through this struggle with you, ask yourself one question: If you could overcome this on your own, why haven't you?

Remember that God gives a certain space for repentance before He allows a catastrophe to come as an intervention. But if need be, God eventually lifts His protective hand and will allow tragedy if it's necessary for a person's restoration. Now may be your "space for repentance," a time for changing the status quo, not maintaining it. But don't delude yourself into assuming that this grace period will go on indefinitely. It didn't go on indefinitely for the world in Noah's time, nor for the cities of Sodom and Ninevah. Nor will it for you. God is still no respecter of persons.

Abandoning the Faith

By now you may be contemplating a complete departure from Christianity. Having tried for perhaps years to overcome homosexual desires, you may feel that the struggle is ferocious and the payoffs minimal. Backsliding looks like the only option left, because it seems you ultimately have to choose between being a homosexual and being a Christian.

Of course, such reasoning is faulty. *All* Christians deal with sin, *all* Christians have stubborn areas of weakness, and *all* Christians at times feel overwhelmed by their personal issues. (Don't forget Paul's "O wretched man that I am!" lamentation in Romans 7.) Yet all Christians don't feel as though they must either completely overcome their weaknesses or else abandon the faith.

Still, it may seem to you that homosexual longings are in a problem class of their own, immune to your best efforts. That being the case, you may think that your only hope of fulfillment lies in leaving Christ and embracing homosexuality because, God knows, you've tried to change but you just can't.

The immediate payoff for such a decision is gratification. You may be able to find some satisfaction in a homosexual relationship, perhaps for a season, perhaps longer. It is useless to paint a morbid picture of such relationships just for the sake of dissuading you—you'll find out for yourself. The point here is that, should you backslide and indulge your passions, you will no longer be denying yourself the "right" to do what seems natural to you. And that may truly seem more important to you than Christianity itself.

But then, what really *is* your concept of Christianity? Before you consider abandoning it, consider whether you really understood it in the first place. Crucial to your understanding is the way you might answer the following questions.

Did God promise you that, having been converted, you would be finished with personal struggles? Was there anything in Christ's teaching implying total fulfillment in this life? Is Christianity a religious form of therapy designed to ensure the happiness of its followers?

Does it make you angry to even ask these questions? If so, you may have forgotten that the core of our faith is the Person Jesus Christ, and the expression of our faith is a life of service to Him, not ourselves.

Francis Schaeffer describes the Christian life in terms of "positives" and "negatives" in his thoughtful book *True Spirituality* (Tyndale House, 1971). Schaeffer feels that, before considering the more "positive" aspects of the faith, we need to identify ourselves with Christ in His death ("not my will but Thine be done") as well as His resurrection—the "negative" preceding the "positive." This principle especially holds true when applied to homosexuality and healing. It seems that people attracted to the same sex experience three common phases after their conversion: an initial phase of idealism ("I'm free! It's all in the past!"), a disturbing plateau during which lingering sexual issues make themselves known ("I'm waiting for my deliverance"), and a period of disillusionment ("So where's the deliverance? Will I ever really change?"). That is the point at which crucial decisions are made, and it is at *that* point, I feel, that identification with Christ's death and a commitment to godly living in spite of unresolved sexual issues must take priority over the desire for change. Only then does real change come—when the desire for it is secondary to the desire to obey.

In short, Christianity is not something you "try" to see if it solves your problems. It is a personal relationship with God made available through Christ, and it is evidenced by a willingness to serve Him on His terms, not ours:

> If anyone desires to come after Me, let him deny himself, and take up his cross, and follow Me (Matthew 16:24).

Regarding our attitude toward this primary but overlooked aspect of Christianity, Schaeffer comments:

> So I must ask, very gently: How much thought does [our identification with Christ's death] provoke? Is it not true that our thoughts, our prayers for ourselves and those we love, are almost entirely aimed at getting rid of the negative, at any cost—rather than praying that the negatives might be faced in the proper attitude?[4]

Regarding sexual practices, he becomes even more specific:

> Here, in the midst of life, there is to be a strong negative, by choice, and by the grace of God. It is not, for example, a matter of waiting until we no longer have strong sexual desires,

but rather that in the midst of the moving of life, surrounded by a world that grabs everything, we are to understand what Jesus means when He talks about denying ourselves that which is not rightfully ours.[5]

We shouldn't leave it at that. There *is* more to Christianity than "the negatives." Infinitely more, beginning with the eternal life that we enter into at the moment of salvation and the honor of knowing and loving God, an honor that must cause us real shame when we consider our preoccupation with our temporary struggles. Inherent in our relationship with God is the privilege of addressing our needs to a loving Father (Matthew 6:7,8), who gives us either the things we request or the grace to deal with our lack (2 Corinthians 12:8,9). So of course a morbid preoccupation with self-denial is not desirable. In fact, it can become idolatrous as an obsession with self-fulfillment. But Schaeffer's point is worth our attention. True fulfillment for the Christian can come only after a surrender of ourselves to God's larger purposes and a commitment to holy living, whether or not it comes "naturally" to us. That is Christian living. If you're going to abandon it, at least know what it is you're abandoning. You're not walking away from a God who let you down; you're probably walking away from a faith you misunderstood.

One more point to consider: Abandoning the faith in a quest for personal happiness may well be the way to sabotage that very quest. Remember that, if you are a believer, you have experienced the rebirth described in John 3, which is not easily shrugged off. You were given the seed of God Himself:

> Having been born again, not of corruptible seed but incorruptible, through the word of God (1 Peter 1:23).

This generates a new nature:

> If anyone is in Christ, he is a new creation;
> old things have passed away; behold, all things
> have become new (2 Corinthians 5:17).

This in turn cannot be fulfilled when violating God's own standards:

> How shall we who died to sin live any longer
> in it? (Romans 6:2).

That being the case, it is questionable whether you will ever be happy in a backslidden state. The dissatisfaction you will feel apart from fellowship with Christ may well outweigh whatever dissatisfaction you're experiencing now as a struggling Christian. You might argue, "But I am who I am—a homosexual. That's my nature, and I can't be at peace unless I'm true to myself."

I would argue the same point, changing the noun. You are indeed who you are—a Christian. That's your nature, and you can't be at peace unless you're true to yourself.

Compromising Scriptural Standards

The past two decades have witnessed a form of compromise that has generated confusion and controversy in equal proportions. Promoters of this option insist that the traditional biblical view of homosexuality is obsolete, and should be replaced with a reevaluation of Scripture which yields, in essence, the following conclusion.

1. There is no biblical condemnation of homosexual behavior so long as it occurs within the boundaries of a "loving, committed relationship."

2. Scriptures commonly supposed to condemn homosexual acts instead condemn only homosexual *lust* or *irresponsible* homosexual behavior.

3. The words commonly translated to mean "homosexual" are generally mistranslated and should be taken to mean either "idolaters," "homosexual prostitutes," or "cowardly people." (See Appendix, "Answering the Pro-Gay Theology" for a more detailed discussion of the Bible and homosexuality.)

The option opened up by such beliefs is to fully accept and act upon homosexual desires *and* remain a Bible-believing Christian, fellowship in a church that openly celebrates gay unions (there are many such churches), and continue to identify yourself as a born-again Christian.

In a sense, this new option isn't new at all. In Revelation 2:14-16 Jesus rebuked the church at Pergamos for holding to the "doctrine of Balaam," claiming to hold that against them. Essentially, this doctrine is derived from the events described in Numbers 22 and 31, in which the prophet Balaam, unable to curse God's people Israel, instead counseled them to compromise themselves through sexual immorality with the Moabites. They retained their identification as God's people, it should be noted, but their compromised holiness had serious repercussions. Jesus identified the believers at Pergamos as being His people, even commending them for their strong points (Revelation 2:13). But the issue was compromise, something which was unacceptable to the Head of the church (Revelation 2:16).

But to other segments of the church and society it is perfectly acceptable. If you have not yet considered this option, be assured that at some point it will present itself to you. Before accepting it at face value, consider the short-term benefits in light of the long-range consequences.

An immediate benefit is the sense of having what looks like the best of both worlds—an openly gay identity (no more struggle!) *plus* a fellowship of believers supporting and even celebrating the very thing you've sought so long to deny. That in itself can be such a powerful experience that it may lead you to believe it's a literal godsend.

It is also possible that your relationship with God will remain intact. (Although your *fellowship* with Him will be seriously injured, in my opinion.) The very notion that a person could affirm homosexuality and remain saved may raise some eyebrows, but it really shouldn't. Remember that the Corinthian believers, in spite of remarkable ungodliness (incest, drunkenness during communion, serious factions) still enjoyed a manifestation of the Holy Spirit in their assembly (1 Corinthians 12 and 14). So you, if you choose this option, may still enjoy a measure of spiritual experience and gifts which are, after all, given without change of mind on God's part (Romans 11:29). Perhaps that too will convince you of the rightness of your choice.

The serious drawback to this option lies in its misrepresentation of Scripture and its unwillingness to accept scriptural authority as absolute. A telling illustration is provided in a pro-gay autobiography which chronicles the expansion of the Metropolitan Community Churches. Explaining his church's interpretation of the Bible and the factors influencing that interpretation, the author states:

> What influences led us to new ways of understanding Scriptures? New scientific information, social changes and personal experience are perhaps the greatest forces for change in

the way we interpret the Bible and develop our beliefs.[6]

To this Francis Schaeffer in *The Great Evangelical Disaster* aptly replies:

> First one starts questioning, based on what the world around us is saying, then one looks at Scripture, then theology, then scientific study—until finally what the Scriptures teach is completely subjected to whatever view is currently accepted by the world.[7]

It is impossible to tamper with one portion of Scripture without compromising all of it. This is not just an academic problem, but a dangerous error that can only lead to further compromise in all areas of life and doctrine.

To choose this option is to do more than accept an altered interpretation of Scripture. It is to participate in deception, and ultimately to become its victim. The compromise that paves the way for deception never stops at one issue, but is characterized by a continued hardening of the heart. And make no mistake about this: No believer, however earnest, is immune to deception and eventual catastrophe when he allows compromise to go unchecked. King Solomon's revelation of God was notable, his calling as King verified by specific visitations. But he had his weaknesses, turning his heart toward lovers who worshiped other gods and who would eventually turn his heart from Jehovah (1 Kings 11:1-8). It would seem as though his idolatry began with simple compromise in one area—liaisons with the ungodly—which grew into overt rebellion. Compromise, idolatry, apostasy. In Scripture, as in life, no downhill course is complete until the bottom is reached.

You are here, you are not alone, and you are facing alternatives. You can't make intelligent choices without dealing with them. If your choice is the option detailed in this book—repentance of all homosexual activity and earnest seeking for sexual wholeness—know that it is in many ways a difficult one. Difficult and wonderful, because your willingness to deal with your sexuality will increase your understanding of so many human issues. Most important, as one who was given the responsibility to steward his body and soul and who did so to the best of his ability, you become a candidate for a blessed pronouncement that few will hear:

"Well done, thou good and faithful servant; thou hast been faithful over a few things, I will make thee ruler over many things; enter thou into the joy of thy Lord" (Matthew 25:21 KJV).

2

Motivation and Expectations

For which of you, intending to build a tower, sitteth not down first, and counteth the cost, whether he have sufficient to finish it? Lest haply, after he hath laid the foundation, and is able to finish it, all that behold it begin to mock him saying, This man began to build, and was not able to finish.

—Luke 14:28-30

One of my first questions to a counselee wanting to change is "Why?" Sometimes that earns me a "Dumb question, buddy" kind of look. "I'm a Christian," is the usual answer, "and Christians aren't supposed to be gay! Isn't it obvious why I want to change?"

Not necessarily. The fact that someone wants to do the right thing doesn't mean they want to do it for the right reason. Proper motivation is essential to success.

Plenty of Christians want to do the right thing for the wrong reasons. Some of us are driven to evangelize friends and co-workers out of a sense of guilt ("Good Christians witness, you know!") rather than out of concern for their souls. Lots of us tithe for a tax write-off, dropping our checks into the offering plate with no thought toward God. And how many pastors are motivated by a need for recognition rather than a love for their flock? Doing the right thing is one matter; *why* you're doing it is another.

37

You might argue that your reason for wanting to change is irrelevant, because your desire to change is enough to guarantee success. Not so. Your motivation needs to be clarified now, at the beginning, because it will determine your consistency and perseverance along the way. Suppose you knew two men who were 40 pounds overweight. Both of them decided to diet, but for different reasons: One wants to look better, while the other has a heart condition and has been warned by his doctor that his life is endangered by his obesity. They both want to do the same thing, but different factors are motivating them. Who are you going to put your money on?

Let me put it more plainly. I've seen plenty of people decide they want to "go straight." Thank God, I've seen plenty of successes. But there are plenty of failures, too. And among the failures I've seen two common elements: wrong motivation and unrealistic expectations.

A Poor Prognosis

A prognosis is the prospect of recovery, whether physical or emotional. It is made by the person treating a certain condition, who bases his prognosis on several factors, including the normal course of the condition, special circumstances, past history, and so forth. So a physician, when asked to give a prognosis for a patient with terminal cancer, will probably give a poor prognosis, meaning that the prospect of recovery is slim.

In counseling, I consider motivation (among many other things) when making a prognosis. In all cases motives are important, but I pay special attention to the reasons people say they want help with homosexuality. Opening statements in counseling sessions say a lot, often revealing the real reason(s) the counselee came in.

"*I'm here for my parents.*"

Always a bad sign, especially since the statement usually comes from an adult. Often, well-meaning parents send their adult daughters or sons into counseling because they (the parents) want their kids to get "straightened out." The kids themselves may be perfectly satisfied with their orientation, but they don't want to upset their families. Or they're afraid of being written out of their parents' wills. Or their parents are putting them through college, and they don't want to jeapordize future tuition payments. And so, under mild (or blatant) coercion, these young men and women come to counseling saying, in essence, "I don't mind being homosexual, but my parents can't stand it, so here I am!"

Now, I'm not unsympathetic to the feelings of parents who find out about their offspring's homosexuality (see Chapter 15). The discovery is usually a shock, creating upheaval and heartache. But nobody can expect to change just because someone else wants them to. And, in my opinion, nobody should even attempt this sort of change if their heart isn't in it.

So let me ask you candidly: Who are you doing this for? Do you, personally, feel that homosexuality is unnatural, that you cannot be satisfied with your sexual leanings, and that to act on them would cause you guilt because you believe such actions are wrong? If not, reexamine your own beliefs and make your own decision. You cannot expect any measure of success unless you yourself want to change.

"*I'm afraid of going to hell.*"

Hell is something to fear, to be sure. It is a literal, specific horror which Jesus warned us about in graphic detail. You can't take the Bible seriously without feeling a certain dread and sadness when the subject of hell comes up.

But homosexuality is not a "heaven or hell" issue. Nobody goes to heaven because they are heterosexual; nobody goes to hell because they are homosexual. Eternal judgment is based on one thing: whether or not your name is recorded in the Book of Life to be opened at the last judgment (Revelation 20:1-15). Through faith in Christ apart from our own righteousness, we can expect to see our names on the record. Whoever will, as Paul said, confess Jesus Christ with their mouth and believe in his heart that God has raised Him from the dead will be saved (Romans 10:9).

A "reformed homosexual" is no more a candidate for heaven than a drug addict who gives up dope or a thief who quits stealing. While all of these are good, admirable reforms, neither they nor any works of righteousness we do can bring us one whit closer to glory. It is Christ's work alone which made provision for our salvation, not any reformation on our part. If you fear hell, go back to the basics:

> God so loved the world that He gave His only begotten Son, that whoever believes in Him should not perish but have everlasting life (John 3:16).

Even after we've been born again into that eternal life, we remain in earthly bodies with earthly struggles. The question for the Christian, then, isn't whether or not his struggles will doom him to hell (they won't), but rather how he can best overcome his struggles because, as a child of God, he has been born to higher purposes.

Many would cite 1 Corinthians 6:9,10 as proof that homosexual behavior condemns anyone who participates, believers included, to hell:

> Do not be deceived. Neither fornicators, nor

idolators, nor adulterers, nor homosexuals...
shall inherit the kingdom of God.

At first glance it would appear that this interpretation of the text is correct. But in the context of this passage, Paul is comparing believers to nonbelievers by describing actions that are common to the nonbeliever (sexual immorality, theft, drunkenness) but uncharacteristic of a Christian. He is not saying that no Christian could ever commit such sins, nor that to do so would condemn even a Christian to hell. He is only pointing out that nonbelievers behave a certain way; believers are expected to behave differently in matters of law, purity, and temperance. A boy may act like a dog by biting another child, and his father might reprimand him saying, "Don't you know that dogs bite people, little boys don't?" The father isn't saying, "Since you've acted like a dog, you are no longer my son. Now you *are* a dog!" Just the opposite. He's saying "Because you are my son, I expect you to act like it!"

If you are a child of God, you're not going to hell regardless of your struggles or your sin. Don't "go straight" to try to become a child of God; rather, abandon sin because you already are a child of God.

Homosexuality, then, sends no one to hell. Does that mean the believer can indulge in homosexual behavior because, no matter what, he remains a child of God and won't be eternally punished for it? Never; just the opposite, in fact. A true believer cannot continue willfully in any sin without suffering consequences. Willful sin goes against the true nature of anyone belonging to Christ (Romans 6:1-4) and can only lead to misery in the long run. But to give up any sin for the sake of avoiding hell is to miss the main point: Through Christ, God has already made provision for us to escape hell in spite of our sins. We overcome sin, then, out of gratitude to and love for God, not to avoid His eternal judgment.

> *"I want to try going straight
> to see if it works."*

And what if it doesn't "work"? Are you saying that either way of life would be okay with you; you'd "prefer" heterosexuality, but you're keeping the homosexual option open? In that case, your interest in change sounds more like an experiment than a commitment. And commitment, not curious dabbling, is needed before any major changes can happen.

Ethics, Beliefs, and Motivation

Which brings us to a proper and reasonable motivation: a desire to change based on ethics and beliefs, and a commitment to abstain from what is known to be unethical and seek what is known to be healthy and right.

All arguments for or against homosexuality get down to questions of ethics: Is homosexuality normal or abnormal, moral or immoral, an orientation God intended for some people or a perversion of normal sexuality?

We are prone to back ourselves into corners when we stray beyond these questions, or when we have no objective standard to answer them by. For example, the conservative who argues that "homosexuality is obviously abnormal because homosexuals are promiscuous, irrational, and violent people" is setting himself up to get shot down. It can be proved that many homosexuals are not promiscuous, and that violence and irrational behavior are common to all people, homosexual and heterosexual alike. So his argument loses its strength because it's based on a debatable point. The question is not whether a person can be nice, responsible, and lovable while being homosexual (a person can, of course, and many gays are very likeable people), but whether or not homosexuality is normal *in and of itself,* and whether or not homosexual acts *in and of themselves* are ever moral.

To answer this question requires an analysis of beliefs about sexuality in general, and a determination of what we base our beliefs on. If we have no objective standard to judge these things by, then arguments against homosexuality are weak. If morality is relative, after all, why shouldn't consenting adults do as they please with either sex? Who's to say that attractions to the same sex are unhealthy if there is no objective standard of healthy sexuality? For that matter, who's to say what the "Christian" view is if there's not even an objective standard for Christian beliefs?

Of course, such a standard exists in the Bible, which is the final test on all matters of belief and morality. The Bible provides concrete answers that are not subject to change or reinterpretation. That's how beliefs and ethics are defined: I believe a thing to be right or wrong, moral or immoral, based on the biblical viewpoint of it. That finally determines what practices and kinds of relationships I can engage in.

If homosexuality is defined as *unnatural* in the Scriptures (it is—check Romans 1), then if I experience homosexual desires I must conclude they are unnatural even if they *feel* natural to me. Any number of abnormalities may feel natural. If we have no standard other than our feelings, then any mood or proclivity we experience can be called "normal."

If homosexual acts are described as immoral in the Scriptures (as they are in Romans 1 and 1 Corinthians 6), then I have to conclude that any form of homosexual behavior, whether in the context of a one-night stand or a 30-year monogamous relationship, is immoral no matter how right or good the behavior may seem. Again, the standard is Scripture, not experience or feelings.

And if I am a Christian, I cannot allow unnatural tendencies or immoral actions to dominate my life. Otherwise I can never be truly at peace, nor can I reach my potential in Christ.

Motivation that lends itself to a good prognosis, then, might be articulated as follows:

> Because I believe, based on biblical standards, that my homosexual desires are unnatural and that homosexual behavior is immoral, and because I know that to continue in any form of immorality will displease the God I love while inhibiting my spiritual and emotional growth, I am committed to abstaining from homosexual acts and am equally committed to doing anything I can to become sexually whole.

Great Expectations

Having made that commitment, what sort of changes can you expect to happen?

Expectations, like motivation, have much to do with success. When people expect too much too soon, they become disillusioned and quit. So let me emphasize the importance of being realistic. Hopeful, yes. Confident in God's work in you, definitely. But never naive or blindly optimistic. I stress this because so many Fighters are plagued by magical thinking. They assume that, having done all the "right things," their sexual struggles will vanish and normal attractions will take their place. Completely. By Tuesday.

Compounding the problem, they may tell themselves that they're healed long before their healing is a reality, supposing that presumption is faith. With a Christian Science sort of mentality they repeat their mantra: "I'm changed, I'm delivered, I'm straight." And when they're sexually tempted they say, "That's not a homosexual desire, it's just a lie of the devil." Their intentions are good, but their theology allows no room for slow growth. When they're finally weary of telling themselves that what *is* really *is not*, they give up the fight.

Don't let that be said of you. Define your expectations, keeping them reasonable and biblically based.

So what sort of changes can you expect? Let's break the subject down by addressing the questions most Fighters pose.

Is it possible for a person who's attracted to the same sex to ever be completely free of those attractions and never experience them again?

Certainly it's possible. But that's not a guarantee that you'll never experience them again. The same can be said of any human tendencies. We all come to Christ with a variety of psychological problems. We commit ourselves to discipleship, trusting in the process of sanctification to bring us closer and closer to His image. As Paul said:

> We all, with unveiled face, beholding as in a mirror the glory of the Lord, are being transformed into the same image from glory to glory, just as by the Spirit of the Lord (2 Corinthians 3:18).

From glory to glory—that's process. Further on he says:

> We who are in this tent (our earthly bodies) groan, being burdened (2 Corinthians 5:4).

There's *struggle* during the process, no question about it. Does that mean we never change? Of course not; we change significantly. The power that our sins have had over us is broken; we no longer have to give in to them. Their influence over us is felt less and less; it is present, perhaps, but not predominant. Our perspective changes as we realize that we are living with the hope of eternal life and that although we are beset by sin to some degree, we are no longer its slaves. These are principles that apply to all Christians, no matter what problems they battle.

Homosexuality is no different. Like all sinful tendencies, homosexual attractions need not rule you or continue to be a predominant force in your life. Specifically, you can expect change to occur in one or all of four ways.

1. *Change in behavior.* Some people argue that behavioral change isn't really change at all. But they're wrong. When a person's behavior changes, his life changes. If a man has been a drunkard for 20 years, then joins Alcoholics Anonymous and stays sober, he has definitely changed. His sobriety will have an impact on all parts of his life, improving his attitude, relationships, and job performance. Will an occasional desire for a drink nullify his claim to have changed? Hardly. So it is with the Fighter. If you've been homosexually active and reach a point of consistent sexual sobriety, you'll have changed. Conscience, confidence, and self control will all have been affected by your abstinence. There's no area of your life that will not feel the impact of it.

2. *Change in frequency of homosexual attractions.* One of the first noticeable changes my clients report has to do with the frequency of their attractions. Over 70 percent of them have stated that they are less often aroused by the same sex. They don't deny that it may still happen, but not nearly as much as it used to. And they're not walking around with their eyes closed, either. Their episodes of attraction to other men are

significantly rarer than they used to be. You can realistically expect, then, to experience a reduction in the frequency of homosexual longings.

3. *Change in intensity of homosexual attractions.* Attractions will become less powerful, less intense, and easier to shrug off. That too is a major change. One male client put it this way:

> I used to be overwhelmed with lust when I'd see a good-looking guy. Now I look, and I'll notice the fact that he's handsome, but I don't feel nearly as turned on as I used to. If I do get aroused, which happens less and less, it's not so strong. It used to be "WOW!" Now it's "oh."

4. *Change in perspective.* Some people are so obsessed with their homosexuality that their obsession is a bigger problem than their attractions. Healing, for these people, begins when they realize that same-sex lust isn't the end of the world. They see it for what it really is—just another manifestation of the fallen nature. The difference between obsession with homosexuality and acknowledgment of it as a nuisance, perhaps, but not a catastrophe, is a change you can also expect to happen.

I would be remiss not to include the testimonies of those who experience no homosexual temptations, ever, to any degree. Such people exist. For most Fighters, homosexuality is reduced from a major issue into a minor one, a problem that does not dominate their lives or keep them from experiencing healthy friendships, healthy marriage, and peace of mind. If it is still a problem to them, it's only one of many; they don't struggle with it daily and they seldom give it serious thought. For them, the battle is not even considered a battle anymore.

Is is possible for someone like me to ever have sexual attractions to the opposite sex?

Yes, it's possible. But the probability of heterosexual desires either emerging or returning depends, to a large extent on your sexual history. Some people have always been exclusively homosexual, never having had attractions to the opposite sex. Others have had, to different degrees, heterosexual attractions which have coexisted with homosexual ones. Of course, the person who has had heterosexual attractions in the past is more *likely* to experience them than the person who has never experienced them in the first place. But even that may be an oversimplification. There are studies which report remarkable changes in orientation, even among those who were predominantly homosexual (see Chapter 6). So in general, yes, heterosexual attractions are possible. (My opinion is that the potential for heterosexuality, like the potential for homosexuality, exists in all people, so that heterosexual response can be awakened in even a predominantly homosexual person.)

Once I do experience changes, would it ever be possible for me to go back into homosexual relationships?

Yes. We can all go back to wherever we've been. Under certain circumstances, anyone can regress, or backslide. That doesn't mean you'll be forever hanging onto your sexual wholeness for dear life. It just means that, like anyone else, you can go backward or forward. That doesn't mean your changes weren't real.

Look at Peter's life. He careened from cowardliness to boldness at different times. He was quite the warrior when he swore he would never deny Christ, and even more so when the soldiers arrested Jesus in the garden and Peter drew his sword, whacking off one of the soldier's ears. His aggression was short-lived, however, when that same night he pretended not even to know

Christ rather than risk his own arrest through association with Him. Then he flip-flopped again in the book of Acts, boldly accusing the people in Jerusalem of murdering Christ, the same people he evidently feared earlier. When he was cowardly, did that mean he was never really bold? Of course not. But in some situations he became weak and regressed.

So can you. I'm convinced that anyone who has had homosexual experiences can, under certain conditions, be homosexually tempted. That doesn't mean such a person *will* be tempted. Some people who have been homosexually oriented in the past later have no attractions at all to the same sex and no desire for any kind of homosexual contact. But the possibility of those desires returning later in life is always there. To expect differently is to be very unrealistic indeed. However, the more you grow, the less likely such a regression will be.

Expect to grow. Expect your homosexual desires to diminish, in both their frequency and their intensity. Expect your perspective to change radically as you expand your vision and reach your potential. These expectations form a proper, realistic, and hopeful viewpoint of the growth process. Combined with a motivation born of love and dissatisfaction with anything less than God's best, they provide you with the inner resources you'll be needing.

Defining your motives and expectations make the process easier. So far we've examined inward issues— beliefs, influences and so forth. Now is the time to begin taking action.

PART TWO

The Struggle to Turn

3

Repentance

Did sin ever yield real pleasure? If so, go back to your old drudgery, and wear the chain again, if it delights you. But inasmuch as sin did never give you what it promised to bestow, but deluded you with lies, be free.

—Charles Spurgeon

When you're angry enough, scared enough, or frustrated enough, you take action. So it is with homosexuality. If you're ready to repent of homosexual sin, it's because you're angry ("I've had it!") scared, ("God be merciful to me a sinner!"), or feeling the futility of it all ("There's nothing in this for me!"). All of those roads lead to repentance.

To repent is to turn. That's what distinguishes repentance from confession, which is a simple acknowledgment of sin as opposed to actively turning from it. It is through confession, according to John 1:9, that we are forgiven of sin:

> If we confess our sins, He is faithful and just
> to forgive us our sins and to cleanse us from all
> unrighteousness.

But confession doesn't necessarily change us, important as it is. God not only calls us to acknowledge our

53

sin; He also commands us to put it away.

Now "repent" is a word we associate with loony old men in sackcloth warning us about the coming doom. (Thanks again, Hollywood.) That's too bad, because repentance is a valuable concept. It means "to think differently, reconsider, turn around." No real changes are made without it. Repentance is the willful act of discontinuing a thing which is destructive, followed by an earnest effort to do what is constructive and right.

Without confession nothing is forgiven, but without repentance nothing is changed.

Repent of What?

To repent, or turn, you need to first identify what you're repenting of, then determine the most effective way to do it. Exactly what do you need to repent of? That depends on exactly how you are expressing homosexual desires.

Of course, you can't repent of *having* those desires. You can't rip them out and abandon them, and you can't just will them away. Repentance applies only to acts of the *conscious will*, whether they are outward actions or inward indulgences. So you are not trying to repent of *homosexuality per se* but of *conscious homosexual expressions*.

Outward expressions of homosexuality include sexual contact, erotic noncontact behavior (exhibitionism, telephone sex), and the use of pornography. These are direct forms of immoral behavior, easy to detect and obviously immoral.

Less obvious but also immoral are indirect expressions, such as conscious lusting or sexual fantasies. Although these practices are inward, they are still conscious expressions, since they involve an act of the will. Conscious lusting is the indulgence of sexual desires for another person. It should be distinguished from an attraction, although the line which distinguishes the two is indeed a fine one. An attraction occurs when a person gets your attention, arouses you, and causes an erotic response. ("Wow, that guy's good-looking; he turns me on"; etc.) Lust, on the other hand, occurs when you feed that attraction by focusing on it, elaborating on it ("I'd love to do this or that with him") or, as some say, "Undressing him with your eyes." To be attracted is no sin; to deliberately fuel that attraction is.

Sexual fantasies are similar. They, like sexual lust, are conscious acts of the imagination. And they too need to be distinguished from fleeting sexual thoughts. Martin Luther, speaking of impure thoughts, said that we can't keep the birds from flying over our heads, but we can keep them from building a nest in our hair. That's pretty well put. Wayward sexual thoughts come to everyone, I suppose, but when we indulge those thoughts by orchestrating sexual fantasies, then we're not just having fleeting thoughts; we're creating mental pornographic home movies.

All of these forms of homosexuality are so obvious that you probably didn't need me to point them out to you.

But repentance shouldn't stop with them. You should also consider any activities that contribute to them or encourage them. Here you need to be very honest with yourself. Are there parts of your lifestyle—habits, places you like to go, forms of recreation—that encourage sexual immorality? (Inward or outward?) That's a question every Christian has to ask himself; it's a question that's doubly pertinent to you. So many Fighters go on kidding themselves, then wonder why they're not making any progress. They claim to want freedom, and seem willing to give up overt homosexual activity, but show an unwillingness to give up the very things that lead them back into that activity.

Bars and nightclubs are a good example. The Bible doesn't specifically say "Thou shalt not go to a bar." And I guess it's possible to attend these places without doing anything overtly wrong. But how does the atmosphere there affect you? Does it stimulate lust, weaken your resolve, put you in an erotic frame of mind? The question should never be "Is going to such and such a place a sin?" but rather "Do I have the liberty to go to this place without setting myself up to stumble? Will it encourage me toward my goals, or will it encourage me toward a setback?"

Health clubs are another sore point for many people. Of course, there's nothing wrong with working out at a spa. In fact, it's a pretty healthy thing to do—but only if you can maintain your integrity while you do it. Plenty of Fighters can barely (if at all) handle the atmosphere at a gym—the communal showers, the steambaths, the groups of naked bodies—without going into acute lust or, worse yet, getting into a sexual encounter. Again, the question isn't whether or not the thing itself is wrong, but whether or not it's wrong *for you*. "All things are lawful for me," Paul said, "but all things are not *helpful*" (1 Corinthians 6:12). In other words, like anyone serious about fulfilling a purpose, Paul weighed his actions against the effect they would have on his life goals. So should you. Bring every part of your life under scrutiny. If anything you're involved with draws you toward the very thing you're trying to outgrow, drop it. Get rid of it. Repent.

Stumbling Blocks to Repentance

There are two major stumbling blocks to repentance that you'll have to fight: the love of the familiar and the fear of the unknown.

Jesus makes an interesting reference to the love of the familiar when He refers to Himself as the "light which came into the world." People, He said, were in darkness and unable to comprehend the light when it came to them. That at least partially explains the rejection of Christ by His own people (John 1:11). But He takes it a step further and says that people were not only *in* darkness but that they actually *loved* it! (John 3:19). Their deeds were evil, and they had no desire to change. The comfort of their present state made them unwilling to consider any other way of life.

Never underestimate the power of the familiar. It has kept countless people from change, even when change would save their very lives. The familiar, after all, may be unhealthy, but at least we know it. We relate to it. And we're all too prone to cling to familiar territory.

When that "familiar territory" is sexual activity, it becomes perversely dear to us. Even though we admit it's wrong, we also come to see it as an old friend. It's reliable and available, and it works. It eases our pain and temporarily satisfies us. To repent of habitual sexual behavior is like abandoning a trustworthy buddy.

Compare this to drug addiction. A person doesn't just fall into it. Somewhere along the line he discovers satisfaction through a chemical. It temporarily eases pain, helps him forget troubles, comforts him. It is his anesthetic, deadening his anxieties like a nurturing parent. Of course there are other ways he could deal with his problems, but the drug is familiar and has a good track record. Why give up something that works?

Meanwhile he is becoming addicted. What began as a comfort is now a necessity, emotionally and physically. To give it up means to go through physical withdrawal, which is hard enough. But it would also mean finding another way to cope with the inner conflicts which remain long after withdrawal. In fact, without the familiar coping mechanism, those conflicts will be stronger and more painful than ever.

The terrible truth, though, is that he *must* find other coping mechanisms, because the one he uses now will eventually destroy him.

God is the author of legitimate need. He created us with the need for intimacy, bonding, love. If we, for whatever reason, do not get these needs met in the normal way, we will develop abnormal ways of satisfying them. Once these abnormal methods are part of our makeup, we're frightened to abandon them. Like faithful old friends, we rely on them and can't imagine doing without them. In that sense we all love the familiar dark, not necessarily for its darkness, but for its familiarity:

> Adult bookstores are always there. You can call 20 of your friends in the middle of the night and they'll all tell you to call back in the morning, but the porno shop doesn't care what time it is. And I always feel comfortable once I get there. Of course, I try to talk myself out of it the whole time I'm driving there, but still, when I'm depressed or feeling lousy, I can go in, look at the bodies, and maybe meet another guy who wants the same thing I do. I know I'll hate myself for it afterward, but that's the way it is. I really need it (male counselee).

Familiarity, no matter how destructive, is hard to abandon. It is the security blanket that smothers our good intentions.

Fear of the unknown is just as tough to beat. When we give up the familiar, we turn toward the unfamiliar. It may be to our benefit to do so, but it still threatens us. The unknown, no matter how good, is still the unknown. We've never been there, so we're not sure what to expect, nor are we certain what to do once we get there. At that point we long again for the comfort of the familiar.

Look at the Jewish people's journey out of Egypt. They had been in a terrible situation, cruelly driven to slave labor by their taskmasters. They lived in bondage and prayed for deliverance, and God intervened. He brought them out of Egypt miraculously and promised them a new start in a good land. And for awhile that sounded great.

Then the exodus, and the problems began. When faced with difficult situations in the wilderness, they were prone to long for the familiarity of Egypt and to dread the unknown Promised Land. Think about the power the familiar held for them! They had been treated worse than animals in Egypt, yet at times they would remember it fondly, saying, "At least we were fed regularly and had our basic needs taken care of!" The unknown frightened them, making them turn toward the bondage that they could at least relate to. And when they finally approached the Promised Land, the terror of its giant inhabitants overshadowed all the benefits that would go along with their new location. In Egypt at least they had survived. How could they be sure they would fare as well in new territory?

If you've met your primary emotional needs through homosexual behavior in the past, you may also wonder how you'll fare in new territory:

> If I could know that someday I'll feel as turned on to a woman as I do to a man, this would be easier. Then it wouldn't be so hard to make all these changes, because I'd know someday it's all going to pay off. But when I look at straight couples and their kids, and think about me living that way and really enjoying it, I can't relate to it. I know where I want to be, but I can't even think of what it

would be like to actually be there. And even if I do get there, how am I going to handle it? (male counselee).

Fruits and Giants

Your love of the familiar (homosexual practices) and fear of the unknown (repentance and a new life) will be alleviated when you consider the joy that the unknown holds for you. Sure, it's tough at times. But it also opens up a way of freedom, new relationships, and peace of mind. The good outweighs the bad immeasurably.

When the Israelites were finally ready to enter the land that God promised to bring them to, they sent out spies to see exactly what their new home would be like. Imagine the anticipation they were feeling! They didn't know much about this place—only that, whatever it was like, it had to be better than Egypt, where they were slaves, or the wilderness, where they were wanderers. So they waited for the spies to return, having told them to bring back a sample of the fruit the land was bearing and a report on the kind of people who were already living there.

The spies returned with good news and bad news. The good news was that the fruit was abundant, a sure sign of healthy land. In fact, the grapes they brought back as a sample were so large that they had to be carried on a staff between two men! There was cause for real optimism, and good reason to charge right in and take over.

The bad news was that there were also huge, intimidating giants dwelling in this unknown territory. The children of Israel appeared to be no match for these guys, who were so big that, according to the spies, they made the average man look like a grasshopper (Numbers 13:17-33). So the unknown held both promise and foreboding. It was wonderful and frightening at the same time. But in the end, the fear of the unknown was finally conquered by the conviction that the land could be—*must* be—entered into.

Fruits and giants—they're part and parcel of the unknown. The fruit of leaving sexual sin is a new and better way of living. But the giants scowl in the background. Loneliness, sexual temptation, misunderstanding from friends, and uncertainty about the future all loom large enough to make you chirp away like a grasshopper. The question is this: Are you going to cling to familiar, destructive ways simply because you can relate to them, or are you willing to abandon them in favor of a new way of living which is better, even though at this point you can't relate to it?

I trust that you're ready and willing to try something better, which means that you're ready and willing to repent.

A Model of Repentance

Second Chronicles chapter 15 lays out an interesting and workable model for repentance. In this account of revival in Israel, King Asa received a message from the prophet Azariah encouraging him to turn his backslidden subjects' hearts back toward the true God. Israel had been without a true priest for some time, and the nation was suffering spiritually without good leadership. Idolatry had become entrenched, and immorality had left the Israelites weakened and restless. King Asa was promised, however, that if he would sincerely seek God his land would be restored.

> When Asa heard these words...he took courage, and removed the abominable idols from all the land of Judah.... Then he gathered all Judah and Benjamin, and those who sojourned with them.... Then they entered a covenant to seek the Lord God of their fathers

with all their heart and with all their soul (verses 8, 9, 12).

Asa responded to the call to repentance in three ways: He took courage, he took sweeping action, and he put everyone on notice that he had made a major decision that would affect all of his people.

1. *Asa took courage.* He needed it! Instituting a national revival was no small undertaking, and it was sure to be met with resistance and misunderstanding. "Why shake everything up?" some of the people no doubt moaned. "We've gotten comfortable with our idols and lifestyle." It required effort and fortitude on Asa's part to stick to his commitment. But he drew courage.

Courage is not an absence of fear; instead, it is a willingness to *do the very thing you're afraid of.* In this case, that willingness comes because you know that you have a divine mandate to repent, just as surely as Asa did. Courage didn't come to him because he knew everyone would applaud his actions. Instead, it came because he knew what he was proposing to do was right. That is your comfort, your source of courage: the knowledge that what you're doing is *right,* and the confident peace that comes with that knowledge.

2. *Asa took sweeping action.* All the idols in Judah and Benjamin were torn down and put away. They weren't stored away for safekeeping, or covered up and hidden; they were put away.

You may never have categorized your sexual sins as "idolatry" because you haven't consciously worshiped them as one would worship an idol. But idolatry needn't include literal worship. To commit idolatry you need only consider a person, activity, or thing to be more important than God. If you allow yourself to habitually indulge in anything that offends God, you are in essence saying that your pleasure is more important than His will. The difficulty of giving something up may cause you such stress and discomfort that you may decide it isn't worth putting yourself through the pain of withdrawal. Sometimes that's the price of righteousness, one which you may consider to be too high. In that case, not only has your sin become an idol, but your *self* has become one as well.

Some people, perhaps you, are literally addicted to sexual activities, and repenting of these activities is no small thing. There *is* such a thing as sexual bondage, or sexual addiction, if you will. I've seen it a number of times, and I'm grateful that this problem in our culture is finally getting the attention it deserves. To be sexually addicted is to literally rely on sex to stabilize you. It's a state in which the rush of sexual pleasure, with all its accompanying chemical forces, has become to you what a drug has become to an addict. And like a drug, it begins to interfere with all parts of life. Breaking the cycle of sexual addiction is not just a matter of will in this case; it's a matter of *strategy, consistency, and patience.* For some people it's a long, exhausting process.

But *repentance* begins that process. Without it there can be no growth, no freedom, no change. And repentance is an act of the will. So the ball is still in your court. Though breaking the patterns of sexual addiction is not *only* an act of the will, it certainly *begins* with an act of the will. (Further strategies for dealing with sexual addiction are mentioned in Chapter 7, "Maintaining Sexual Integrity.")

To put away sexual idolatry, you first need to call it what it is: a form of sexual expression that has come between you and God, one which you're putting away once and for all in response to His command "You shall have no other gods before Me." This creates a new frame of mind, a commitment to stop both the sexual acts and any activities that draw you toward them. It is, as I mentioned earlier, your anger, fear, or sense of futility which will sustain this commitment. All three can be valuable. Anger at the notion of anything controlling you keeps you from coming under its control again. Fear of ultimate consequences—disease, arrest, bondage— gives you the common sense to avoid anything that would draw you back into immorality. And a sense of the futility of sexual sin makes you loath to invest any more time and energy in it. In other words, repentance is evidenced by a changed attitude which expresses itself in concrete actions. You stop the activity and commit yourself to abstaining from it in the future.

3. *Asa put people on notice.* King Asa didn't go sneaking out at night in disguise, tearing down the idols while nobody was looking, and saying, "Shhh! I don't want to offend anyone!" The sins that had been openly committed had to be openly abandoned. This is an important principle too often overlooked by repentant believers: When your particular sin involves other people (as homosexuality usually does), then those same people need to know you've abandoned that sin.

There are practical reasons for this. No matter how sincere you are, you're going to be tempted. That's a reality for all of us. When we're accustomed to getting satisfaction out of something, even when we've decided to give it up, we're drawn back toward it when times get rough.

Ever try dieting? If you have, you know that when you're depressed or frustrated you're especially prone to break your diet. Let's say you're used to eating out with some friends once a week at a pizza parlor. If they don't know you're dieting, won't they expect you to join them in some pizza during your next get-together? And if you're already feeling like breaking your diet anyway, won't it be easier to do so if no one knows you're trying to abstain from pizza?

Granted, there's a major difference between dieting and sex, but the same principle applies: When you abandon sexual sin, you'll find yourself drawn back toward it at some point when you're feeling low. If the people you've been sexually active with don't know about your decision, it will make it that much easier for you to go back to your old patterns of behavior with them.

If you've been involved only in anonymous encounters, you can't very well track your partners down and make an announcement to them. There's no need to, anyway. Likewise, if your expression of homosexuality has been exclusively through fantasies or pornography, there really isn't another person to discuss this with. But if there are people you've been sexually involved with who you're still interacting with, they need to know about your decision. If you don't advise them of it now, you'll just set yourself up for problems later on.

Case in Point: Brad

Brad entered counseling after a recent breakup with his lover. He had gotten into the relationship as a backslidden Christian, and after rededicating himself to the faith, he decided to finally deal with his homosexuality. But two stumbling blocks kept holding him back, both of which he could have avoided if he had only put people on notice. He was still strongly attracted to his ex-lover Jake, and none of his gay friends knew about his decision to give up homosexual activity. As a result, both his friends and his ex-lover expected him to go about his business as usual.

Brad still saw Jake on occasion. Each time he did, he was determined not to have sex with him, but Jake still expected a sexual encounter to cap off their time together, since he had no reason to believe that Brad would object. In spite of his best intentions, once they were alone together Brad couldn't say no. Jake had expectations, Brad had attractions, and the inevitable happened time and again. Finally, instead of relying on sheer willpower, Brad confessed to Jake that he no longer felt homosexuality was an option for him. To his credit, Jake respected Brad's decision, though he disagreed with it, and they decided to keep their relationship nonsexual.

Dealing with his other gay friends was another matter. Brad wanted to avoid being "preachy," but he felt he was being dishonest with them by keeping his decision to himself. They in turn kept trying to play "matchmaker" with him by setting him up with new dates. The situation was getting pretty awkward, to say the least.

We worked out a simple way to discuss the problem with his friends. Since Brad had no intention of forcing his beliefs on them, he decided to tell them, one at a time, that he had come to view homosexual relationships as being incompatible with his faith. He asked each of them if they could continue their friendship with that understanding. Some gladly complied while others took real offense to Brad questioning the validity of homosexuality. But at least the conflict was settled. Brad kept the friendships of those who could respect his right to live as he saw fit, and he continued to show them the same respect.

Some would consider it wrong to maintain relations of any kind with gay friends or ex-lovers, but there's no hard-and-fast rule saying you should simply cut off those who disagree with you. The acid test is always this: If you can maintain a relationship that doesn't compromise your own beliefs, then do so. Discuss your differences, by all means, and be honest about where you stand. Then you can decide which relationships you can maintain, and which ones you'll have to withdraw from.

By now your dissatisfaction with homosexuality should have crystallized into a motivation to change, and your motivation will have led you to take repentant action. You've identified what specifically you've needed to turn from, and you've turned from it and let the appropriate people know about your decision. Your repentance should be manifested by a change in behavior and outlook.

When John the Baptist called the people to repentance, he wasn't just asking for a decision. "Bear fruits worthy of repentance," he exhorted, meaning that tangible evidence always follows a true conversion. For now, the fact that you've turned away from old patterns is a part of that evidence. The next step, turning toward something new, begins when you lay a new foundation for growth.

4

Laying the Foundation

God never intended man to repent of sin for repentance's sake alone. The higher purpose has always been to bring us into a better life. Sin is abhorrent to God because it keeps us from that better life. Without those "better things" to strive for, what's the point in repentance?

Apply this truth to homosexuality and you'll get a clearer picture of God's intentions toward you. You're not called to give up homosexuality just because it's "bad"; you're invited to a life of wholeness which you can't attain as long as you hold on to anything that's second best. Attaining wholeness, though, means growth. And growth cannot come until the things stifling it are abandoned. Repentance of homosexual behavior is just a means to an end, that end being the sexual and emotional health that is your spiritual birthright. That's what you, and God, are fighting for.

Growth requires a solid foundation—a lifestyle—built on principles and actions that allow your growth to flourish. Your task at this point is to lay a foundation that is flexible enough to allow growth, and strong enough to fall back on when you're tested. Believe me, if you don't have a foundation good enough to fall back on, you'll just fall, period.

Houses depend on foundations made of concrete elements, sturdy enough to uphold the building during storms and earthquakes, strong enough to handle additions to the structure. The building process starts with the foundation, and everything that's built afterward stands or falls on that foundation's strength. So it had better be well-planned.

Personal growth is rooted in a solid foundation as well. To build it, you need to establish a lifestyle which regularly strengthens you. That is the best defense I know of against regression, or backsliding. It is also the best way I know of to promote progress. Neglect your foundation, or lay it without forethought, and you set yourself up for failure.

A good foundation is a lifestyle that pays regular attention to the following: spiritual disciplines, church fellowship, emotional support through specialized care, and social resources. These four elements provide structure, and structure is vital. Within it there can be growth and expansion; without it there is only chaos.

Spiritual Disciplines

The essence of your strength lies in your spiritual health, and the essence of true spirituality is an intimate knowledge of God. Without this Christianity is reduced to ritualistic dryness. You cannot hope to be fulfilled by going through the motions of service toward a God you are far from. Now, more than ever, you need to draw near.

Though this is true of all Christians, it's doubly true of you. You're dealing with a tough issue while making major life changes. For you to even attempt this without a solid spiritual base is as foolish as a man attempting to become a championship bodybuilder without the use of his arms. He's not going to pump much iron without those limbs, and you're not going to grow much without spiritual strength.

Spiritual strength comes through routine. Legalistic as that may sound, it's the people who incorporate prayer and Bible study into their routines that exhibit the most success.

That's because we cannot know God without investing time in communication with Him. That's applicable to all relationships, isn't it? We can't say we know someone if we haven't spent time talking to him, listening to him, experiencing closeness with him. And we certainly can't say we love someone who we haven't taken the time to know.

There are plenty of people we interact with daily who we don't really know because we invest no personal time in them. Look at your co-workers, for example. Chances are you spend a good deal of time in their company without knowing their real thoughts or feelings. You're together, but uninvolved. Sadly, we're prone to treat God like a co-worker. We acknowledge His presence but invest no energy in personal communion with Him. We don't know Him, so how can we love Him?

A routine of daily prayer and study goes a long way toward correcting the problem. Incorporate it into your life now.

While doing so, avoid the tendency to take on more than you can handle. People who reestablish their spiritual disciplines are prone to unrealistic zeal, promising themselves and God that they'll spend an hour in prayer daily after reading ten chapters of the Bible. Of course they give up after a few days, going back to no prayer life at all.

You're not a cloistered nun, I assume, so don't try to act like one. Instead, start by setting aside at least 15 minutes daily for reading one chapter of the Bible and praying afterward. You can handle 15 minutes, I don't care what your schedule is like. And if you'll make that a part of your daily routine—no excuses, no sloughing off—you'll see changes, quickly, in all parts of your life.

Why the importance of both prayer and Bible reading? Because they are the two primary tools we use to know God. We listen to Him through His Word, and we speak to Him in prayer.

We're built up in faith by exposure to the Word (Romans 10:17), which cleanses us (John 15:3) and by which we're instructed in righteousness (Psalm 119:9). We communicate our needs through prayer, given the promise that our requests are heard when made according to His will (1 John 5:14,15). Those are general principles applicable to any believer.

There are other reasons you should be diligent in private devotions. Look at the changes you're making. Look at the struggles you're up against. Look at the number of people on one side who don't understand those struggles, then look at the number of people on the other side who think you shouldn't even try to change. Where are you going to find your strength and solace in the middle of all this, if not from God? And how will you ever find that solace in God if you're not willing to invest time and effort in cultivating your relationship with Him?

Another crucial point: How can you ever really know God's thoughts toward you without knowing Him personally? Do you realize that your attitude toward God has everything to do with the attitude you think He has toward you?

Fighters often begin their process feeling alienated from God. They say they feel that way because of something they've done, usually something sexual that they were especially ashamed of. Further examination, though, shows that they felt that way long before they got involved in sexual sin. The sense of alienation from God really began when they began feeling alienated from people in general, especially important authority figures. To them, those figures represent God. That's pretty normal. Jesus used earthly fathers as models of God when He taught, because the illustration of a loving father would help people understand God's attitude toward them. But what if the earthly father is perceived as unloving, impatient, distant? The heavenly Father will be perceived the same way. So a frustrating cycle begins: God is perceived as unloving because other authority figures seem to be unloving. That misconception can only be corrected by getting to know Him as He truly is.

You probably need a better understanding of God and His feelings about you. The wrong perception *of* Him creates the wrong response *to* Him. That can only be corrected by taking the time to know Him through private communicating. Make that a priority.

Church Fellowship

Church fellowship is as crucial to your foundation as private devotions. Hopefully you're already committed to a local church body. But I know there's a good chance you're not, because many people in your situation avoid the church.

The reasons vary. The one I hear most frequently is that the church doesn't understand the needs of a Fighter (quite true, sometimes). Therefore, fellowship won't be of any benefit (quite false, always).

Remember, there are plenty of issues besides yours which most Christians don't understand, and plenty of other issues being mishandled by the church. But the benefit of fellowship isn't derived from being perfectly understood; it's derived from the encouragement and love expressed between believers. That love may be imperfect and the encouragement incomplete, but you can't grow without it. As long as there is a body of Christ, and as long as you're a part of it, you'll need its other members.

Anger with Christians is another reason that many Fighters give for shying away from fellowship. To a point that's understandable. Many Christians (though by no means *all* of them) have treated people like you pretty badly. To hear some of them talk, you would think homosexuality was the worst of all sins, the ultimate abomination (and yet, gossip, pride, and injustice are also cited as abominations in the Bible). And some believers hold such curious notions about homosexuality! Some think you simply chose to have these feelings. Others think you're not really a Christian if you have such feelings. And many would avoid you if they knew about your struggles, as though homosexuality was somehow contagious. So your anger is understandable, even justifiable, to some degree.

But believe it or not, you're in good company. The apostle Paul wasn't much of a saint in his early days. In fact, he was an aggressive, fanatical zealot dedicated to the eradication of Christianity. His zeal took on murderous proportions. He gave an approving nod to the murderers of Stephen, the first Christian martyr, even holding their cloaks for them while they stoned the young man to death. He sought Christians out, dragging them before the religious authorities to have them charged, jailed, and executed. In fact, when he was apprehended by Christ on the road to Damascus, he was in the process of carrying out his violent mission.

Men like that normally develop a bit of a reputation.

Is it any wonder, then that when he became a convert to Christianity, other believers were reluctant to accept him into fellowship? Who could relate to his crimes? Who could be sure that he was sincere? And who wouldn't have just a touch of morbid curiosity about Paul's bloody past?

Like you, Paul was deeply misunderstood. His background haunted him, seeming to close the door on future relationships within the church. In fact, according to Acts 9:26, when he tried to join the believers in Jerusalem, they were afraid of him and doubted his authenticity as a disciple. He could have given up. He could have, with some justification, stomped his foot and said, "Hey, you guys were all sinners just like me, even though we all didn't commit the same sin! Why can't you just accept me as I am? You're not playing fair; I'm outta here!" Of course, to his credit and our benefit, he stuck it out. And, as He always does, God provided Paul with a way out in the form of an understanding soul named Barnabas. Barnabas took a stand for Paul, convincing the other disciples that his conversion was genuine and his intentions good. He extended to Paul the right hand of fellowship which bridged the gap between Paul and the Christians he had been alienated from.

Don't underestimate the entire body of Christ just because of painful experiences you've had with some Christians. Barnabas wasn't the first and last of his kind; there are others who've been cut from the same mold. They often don't stand out, and they may be overshadowed by their less-sensitive brethren. But they exist, and if you refuse to give yourself a chance to encounter them, you'll miss one of Christianity's greatest joys—hearty fellowship—as well as one of the most important sources of healing.

And this brings us to the reason that you, especially, need to participate in a local church body. Homosexuality is a relational problem. It's characterized by a perverse form of sexual relating, and has its origins in some sort of relational difficulties. I am convinced that healthy, intimate relationships are the key toward outgrowing homosexuality. And those relationships are best found among believers. It is the *church* which becomes your prime resource for relationships that build you up, encourage you, and promote your healing. Shun the church and you shun your own healing.

If you're not already in one, it's up to you to seek out a church. Thank God, we're in a nation rich with churches, which means you probably have several in your area to choose from. Naturally, yours needs to be one that upholds the authority of the Bible, preaches orthodox Christianity, and encourages spiritual growth. Give yourself no excuses for putting this off. Fellowship is not optional; it's a basic part of the structure for anyone's growth.

Specialized Care

Now is a good time to look into specialized help from people who have had experience dealing with homosexuality. That kind of help is usually available through professional counseling or specialized ministry, both of which are valuable and should be considered.

Although I include this as one of the four basic parts of a good structure, I should also say that you will, with or without specialized care, continue to grow. Your growth is a process involving you, God, and significant relationships. Professional help or specialized ministry helps the process along, to be sure, but it isn't the process itself. In other words, if such help isn't available, you're still capable of attaining your goals. But if such help is available, why shouldn't you take advantage of it?

Without hesitation, I suggest finding a Christian counselor. You shouldn't feel afraid of professional therapy, though you should approach it carefully. Even Dave Hunt, an outspoken critic of most modern psychology, allows that at times professional counseling can be helpful:

> We are not denying the value of professional counsel for those areas of daily function that are not covered in the Bible and do not find resolution solely through our relationship with God in Christ. In seeking counsel, however, it should always be biblical to the extent that the Bible covers the situation.[1]

There are many qualified Christian therapists who can help you identify conflicts and give proper, godly counsel. It will be to your benefit to look into this. In a professional therapeutic environment you have the freedom to discuss things best left unsaid in other relationships. Your self-perception, fantasy life, sexual urges, and irrational moods can be explored without fear of social repercussion, with a person who is trained to take that information and to correctly analyze it and offer suggestions that are unique to your situation. It gives you an opportunity to know yourself and to understand the roots of your behavior and desires. That alleviates anxiety, which is healing in itself, and it gives you useful information.

Sometimes looking for a therapist can be stressful enough to make you need one. It's hard to know who's best for you, and there is no guarantee, once you've started, that you've found the right one. But there are safeguards you can take to make the search easier.

Get a recommendation, if possible, from your pastor or from someone you know who's been through therapy.

That's always better than picking a name out of the directory.

Find out before your first visit what the therapist's licensing or educational credentials are, whether or not there's a fee for an initial consultation (there usually is), and how much it will cost. Be specific about your needs; if possible, discuss them with the therapist over the phone before coming in. Tell him what you're dealing with and why you're looking for help.

Ask questions. Find out where he stands on homosexuality and Christianity, and specifically how he deals with these issues in therapy. Ask about his prior experience. Has he dealt with this before? How often? What kinds of results does he expect when doing therapy with someone in your position?

Don't pick the first therapist you meet (unless that's the only one you could find). It's better to visit at least three counselors before making a decision to begin therapy. It's a major investment of finances and time, so consider it carefully.

Be sure you feel reasonably comfortable with a therapist before you commit yourself to working with him. "Reasonably comfortable" is a subjective term, I know, and therapy is never comfortable in the beginning anyway. But you should feel as though you're working with someone who knows what he's doing, is respectful of you and your feelings, and displays a genial, professional manner.

You should also consider the finances involved. You'll be in therapy for awhile, so review your budget, check your medical insurance to see if it covers mental health care, and plan accordingly.

I don't believe professional therapy is your only option, nor do I believe that you can't grow and change without it. But if it's feasible economically and good help is available, I urge you to take advantage of it.

Specialized Ministry

Another option is specialized ministry to Christians dealing with homosexuality. If you don't know of any such ministries in your area, contact Exodus International (listed in the back of this book under "Resources") or check with your pastor. These ministries usually function as groups, combining prayer, teaching, and support. Joining up with such a group can alleviate the sense of isolation so common to your kind of struggle and can provide real encouragement from people who face many of the same issues that you do.

The insight you can gain from these groups is especially valuable. You can learn how other people handle temptation or alleviate loneliness. And you get the benefit of learning from other people's mistakes.

You also learn acceptance of the things you cannot change. (There's usually a period of frustration in the early stages of growth.) Change becomes an obsession ("When will I feel differently toward my own sex and the opposite sex?") and patience wears thin. By meeting with people who share your struggles, you'll see how they deal with it. You'll get a better perspective, realizing that although you can't wish the presence of homosexuality away, you can diffuse the anxiety you feel over it.

Be careful, though, not to make a specialized support group your only social outlet. For a time it may be the one place you know of where you can meet people and feel comfortable, but that should be a temporary rather than a long-term situation. Never substitute specialized ministries for the local church body, and never limit your relationships to other support-group members. That will only deepen the feeling that you're different from everyone else, making you feel as though only another "struggler" could relate to you. That leads to narrow friendships, based primarily on a mutual wound, in which the topic of discussion is usually homosexuality and healing. That's unhealthy, and boring as well. Who wants to talk about *this* all the time?

A specialized ministry should, among other things, teach you better ways of relating so you can establish other friendships outside the group. It's a bridge toward more social integration—a place to heal wounds, gather strength, and move on.

Social Resources

Your resources should include at least one intimate friend (preferably more than one) and some acquaintances.

Intimate friends provide your main source of support. You confide in them and rely on their input to stabilize you. They make you feel important. They prove to you that you're significant, unique, worthwhile. Sometimes their love for you is the one thing that keeps you from despair.

Acquaintances are sometimes looked on as second-rate friendships ("She's not a *friend*, just an *acquaintance*") but they're valuable in their own right. They offer variety and fun. Your interactions with them color your life and broaden your perspective. When you go to parties you see them, lightly interact, and feel refreshed. That too is vital to emotional health.

Social resources—friends and acquaintances—are terribly overlooked and underrated as prime agents of healing. Often when I ask a new counselee what sort of social life he has, he blinks and says, "What's that got to do with homosexuality?"

Plenty. Relationships are your most valuable resources. You've got to know that you are significant to somebody else, appreciated for your gifts and uniqueness. And you've got to know that you have people to lean on, people interested in your life and rooting for you as you grow.

Your relationship with your therapist, pastor, and support-group members will offer you some of those benefits. But you need more. You need to know that you are valued for your total self, not just because you have a problem requiring special care. And that knowledge will only come through friendships. They form a vital part of your foundation.

So take stock. Who are you close to right now as you read this? What friendships do you have that are deep, have some longevity to them, and are dependable? Your close friends are your allies, and allies are crucial. If you have them, nurture them. A good foundation will include regular, planned contact with intimate friends.

Take stock of your acquaintances as well. Keep in touch with them and follow up on those "Let's have lunch" promises. Time spent with acquaintances is relaxing, energizing time. It shouldn't be a rarity. Make it part of your lifestyle.

I'm harping on this friendship/acquaintance concept because I've noticed that counselees who socialize make quicker progress, are less prone to depression, and keep a better attitude. Their contacts keep them buoyant, even when they're dealing with painful emotional issues. Most important, I think, is the effect that friendship has on their self-perception. It literally corrects the false concepts they've grown up with ("I'm different than everyone else, I don't have anything to offer"), proving them to be wrong and changing the way the counselee responds to people in general. That's just the sort of change you need.

If you don't have social resources, you're at a real disadvantage. I urge you to take this to heart: Without friendships you are incomplete. If you have them, strengthen them. If you don't have them, do whatever is necessary to make them. (Chapter 9 will cover some strategies for social integration.)

Foundation-laying requires time management. You need to plan devotions, church attendance, social activities. If you need some help with basic time management and prioritizing, Gordon MacDonald's book *Ordering Your Private World* (Oliver Nelson Publishers, 1984) would be of real use to you. It cuts through the excuses we give for poor planning and gives clear, workable solutions for the confusion of a disorganized private life. While you're at it, if you don't have an appointment book, pick one up. Plan your weeks in advance, blocking out regular time for laying and strengthening your foundation. You may be surprised how much time is really available when it's mapped out beforehand.

Your foundation undergirds your process. It contains the resources that hold you up while you struggle toward growth, so it had better be solid. Once it's laid, though, it requires tending. That's what makes this foundation less like concrete and more like a garden. It needs to be watched and cared for regularly. Any of its elements will decay if they're neglected. So your foundation, like a chain, is only as strong as its weakest point. Build it carefully and watch it constantly!

PART THREE

The Struggle to Know

5

Why Me?

So far we've concentrated on decision-making and integrity, because they lay the foundation that makes growth possible. This is a principle repeated throughout Scripture: God calls a person or a people to obedience, giving them some basic promises, then waiting until they've responded in obedience before revealing more truth. The children of Israel, for example, were told they would be delivered from bondage and brought into a new home. Only after their departure from Egypt (obedience) did God reveal more of Himself through the law and divine guidance. Christ's disciples followed a similar pattern: They were called, they responded, they were taught. And Paul, after his conversion, was given bits and pieces of guidance. Only after obeying God's initial commands did he come into deeper revelations.

It was necessary for you as well to respond first through conformity to God's standards. You repented of homosexual sin (if you were involved in any), then laid a foundation for growth. Now you can enter into a stage of enlightenment. It's time to learn about yourself: to learn what lies behind your homosexual attractions, why they exist, and how they've affected your ability to relate to yourself and others.

We're going to look at some theories on the origins of the homosexual orientation. In so doing, we'll try to answer a fundamental question you've asked yourself hundreds of times: Why me?

Why you, indeed? You never asked for homosexual attractions. You never decided to incorporate them into your sexual makeup. Given the choice, you might have picked any number of problems before choosing this one. As for the conflicts creating your homosexuality, we know you didn't choose those, either. You didn't decide what family you'd be born into, you didn't choose to respond to early events in a given way, and you certainly didn't have anything to say about those responses when they became sexual. You are, in many ways, a victim of circumstance. As far as the development of your attractions to the same sex is concerned, you're blameless. God does not and will not hold that against you. It is not a sin to be homosexually inclined. It's what you *do* with those inclinations that condemns or commends you.

With that in mind, we'll look to two sources to help us understand where it all began: the past, and psychological theories.

Many Christians are reluctant to study their past. After all, "the past" has traditionally been the great scapegoat. "I can't help doing the things I do because such and such happened to me. I'm not really responsible," or so goes the message that many self-analyzed subjects would have us believe. That just isn't true, and that sort of blame-placing should be avoided at all costs. The past, no matter how awful, doesn't force us to behave in certain ways, and we can't duck our culpability in the present by blaming an unhappy childhood or a traumatic event. We alone are responsible for our actions; any philosophy which teaches otherwise should be avoided.

But a look at the past can help us understand our present condition, and can give us useful information with which we can correct our present problems. We can learn from the past and thus improve the present.

Scripture has something to say about this. Much of the Old Testament consists of explanations gleaned from history which help us understand the present. The fall of man, the formation of the Hebrew people, and the victories and failures of the patriarchs are all detailed in the Old Testament. Paul succinctly describes the value of learning about these and other past events by telling us that "all these things happened to them as examples, and they were written for our admonition" (1 Corinthians 10:11). In short, the past helps us to understand the present. And what we understand, we can deal with.

Psychology is another area of controversy among Christians. It needn't be, because the study of human behavior is worthwhile. The book of Proverbs is full of psychological thought, so God clearly commends it when properly used. The fact that much of today's psychology is polluted with anti-Christian teaching should not scare us away from the field itself. It should make us cautious, even skeptical at times, but not unwilling to examine what it has to offer that is of merit. There's nothing wrong with psychological theory per se, unless and until it usurps the authority of the Scriptures or becomes the end-all and be-all solution to human problems.

Here's a simple test to determine whether or not a psychological theory is valid: If it contradicts the Bible, reject it outright. It's false. If it is not spelled out in Scripture, but doesn't contradict it either, at least accept its possibility. It might be true. If it's in the Bible, affirm it as absolute truth. Within these guidelines we'll consider some theories on homosexuality. Our goal here is knowledge, because, as Solomon said, "A wise man is strong; yes, a man of knowledge increases strength" (Proverbs 24:5). Solomon commends learning as strength. And strength makes for good Fighters.

Knowledge also reduces anxiety. Because of the stigma attached to homosexuality, Fighters battle not only their attractions but also intense anxiety because of those attractions. This anxiety leads them to draw false conclusions about themselves that are inaccurate and damaging. They assume it's all somehow their fault. "I'm an unusually rotten person," they figure, "because only a rotten person would have a problem like this." But the more they learn about the nature of homosexuality, the more their anxiety fades. They feel less separated from the rest of humanity, because they realize their sexual desires indicate basic though unfulfilled needs—needs which are similar to everyone else's. The way they've been expressed may not have been normal, but the needs themselves are. It's a relief to learn that.

To better answer the question "Why me?" we'll look at some general theories on the origins of homosexuality, then compare them to the experiences of many Fighters like you.

Biological Theories

These deserve mention, because they answer another question you've probably considered: Was I born this way?

It might seem that way. You may remember feeling "different" from day one. Perhaps you even remember having homosexual fantasies at an early age. And if your struggle has been a long one, you may have wondered if its stubbornness is caused by biological ingredients.

It has been shown that there *may* be biological influences which could *predispose* a person toward homosexuality. The key word here is "predispose," as in "having a tendency toward something." People can be born with predispositions toward any number of problems—depression or alcoholism, for example—yet that doesn't make the problems inevitable. It is the environment which brings them to fruition. The following studies bear this out.

"It is not for psychoanalysis to solve the problem of homosexuality," Freud said. "It must rest content with discovering the psychical mechanisms that resulted in the determination of the object-choice.... There its work ends, and it leaves the rest to biological research" (Sigmund Freud, 1920).

Whether or not they took their cues from Freud, scientists and sex researchers have certainly tried to discover a biological cause for homosexuality. Yet none has been found. There is no biological factor shown to be consistently present in homosexually oriented people.

Prenatal Influences

Research does show that there *may be* prenatal influences on the development of homosexuality in *some* cases, yet these influences do not *determine* homosexuality. Background studies on the mothers of homosexual males, for example, showed in some cases a history of marked stress during their pregnancies. Stress affects the hormone levels of expectant mothers and consequently the hormone levels in the child they're carrying (Dorner, 1987; Ward, 1972, 1984). Dr. John Money and associates at John Hopkins University drew similar conclusions, citing the "Adam/Eve Principle" as an explanation for the effects of hormonal imbalance on the unborn child's brain:

According to the Adam/Eve principle, simply stated, if the fetal brain is not hormonalized, it will develop from its early sexually bipotential stage to be, like Eve, feminine. To be like Adam, it must be hormonalized.[1]

For masculinity to emerge in the fetal brain, Money theorizes, an adequate hormone level is necessary. If that level is disrupted, the brain of a male child will become "feminized" and have inborn feminine characteristics. Other theorists seem to agree (Dorner, 1987; Weinrich, 1987; Wilson 1988).

Genetics

F.J. Kallman and others proposed a theory of genetic origins of homosexuality in a 1952 study of 63 twins (37 identical, 26 fraternal). Although Kallman reported homosexuality as a common phenomenon in the identical twins, other researcher doing similar work with identical twins had different results (Heston and Shields, 1968; Rosenthanl, 1971; Fuller and Thompson, 1978).

Likewise, Dorner (1976) proposed that male homosexuals may have developed a "feminine sexual brain" caused by androgen deficiency, a conclusion he based on a study of "effeminate" homosexual men (see Van Den Aardweg, 1986, for a fuller treatment of Dorner).

Dannemeyer (1989) cites two authorities whose statements are relevant here. If we accept the argument that homosexuality is inborn and therefore normal, we would also have to assume that alcoholism and depression, if proven to be inborn, are likewise normal:

> Chemical events are going on in a number of different ways which will produce alcoholism (Frank Siexas, former Director of the National Council on Alcoholism, quoted in the *Boston Globe*, August 8, 1983).

A low level of serotonin seems to be a bio-chemical marker for those depressed people who are most prone to suicide (Dr. Herman van Praag, Psychiatrist at Albert Einstein College of Medicine, quoted in *New York Times*, October 8, 1985).

If it could be proven that alcoholism and depression were inborn, would we therefore accept them as normal states and refuse to treat them? Does their "predetermined" nature make them healthy? So the arguments for "inborn homosexuality," even if they were proven true, could never be taken as proof that homosexuality is a normal variant of human sexuality.

But have the biological or genetic theories of the origin of homosexuality been proven true? Hardly:

> The child's psychosexual identity is not written, unlearned, in the genetic code, the hormonal system or the nervous system at birth (John Money, *Perspectives in Human Sexuality*, New York Behavioral Publications, 1974, p. 67).

> The genetic theory of homosexuality has been general discarded today... no serious scientist suggests that a simple cause-effect relationship applies (Masters, Brown, and Kolodny, *Human Sexuality*. Boston, Little, Brown and Co., 1984, p. 319-320).

> The idea that people are born into one type of sexual behavior is foolish (John DeCecco, editor of the *Journal of Homosexuality*, quoted in *USA Today*, March 1, 1989, p. 4D).[2]

We're now left facing the multitude of theories about the development of homosexuality. From Freud to the present, theorists have proposed that it can be traced to a dominant mother, a hostile father, an early sexual molestation, a fear of women or men, masturbation, or any combination of the above.

My objection to all these theories is not that they're necessarily wrong, but that they assume each person has homosexual attractions for the same reason. I would argue that, like other problems, its roots vary from individual to individual.

We've got to approach this subject with a respect for the complexity of human sexuality in general. There is much we don't know about sexual preferences and behaviors—how they develop, why they arise in certain people but not in others. So we've got a lot to learn about homosexuality. We don't have all the answers; I'm sure we never will.

Having said that, I will offer a few common patters I've seen in the development of homosexuality. Instead of one universal cause, I've seen a consistent developmental pattern. Specifically, I've come to believe that homosexual attractions develop within a simple process:

1. A child's perception of his or her relationship to parents or significant others.

2. A child's emotional response to those perceptions.

3. Emotional needs arising from these perceptions and responses.

4. The sexualization of those emotional needs.

This pattern allows for a number of child traumas to occur, placing the emphasis not so much on what did or didn't happen but on the way the child perceived it. That explains the variety of childhood histories found among homosexually oriented adults. Some actually had wonderful parents, while some were raised by tyrants. It was their *perception* of their early relationships, not necessarily the facts themselves, that generated a response.

Consider a rather general example. A boy is raised by a father who adores him, spends time with him, and provides well for his family. Then, through circumstances beyond the father's control, he has to take a second job which keeps him away from the home. The boy is too young to understand economic realities; all he knows is that Dad is gone, and he takes that as a personal rejection. It doesn't matter whether or not his father has really rejected him—he *perceives* his father's absence as rejection and responds accordingly. He feels hurt, develops a resentment toward his father, and emotionally withdraws from the person he feels rejected by.

In another family, a girl is raised by a mother who truly dislikes her. She makes no bones about it, telling her daughter that she wishes she'd never been born and that she wants nothing to do with her. This child, too, feels hurt, develops a resentment toward her mother, and emotionally withdraws from the person she feels rejected by.

Two children from completely different backgrounds, both responding to early pain in the same way. Both have experienced disruption in their relationship with the parent of the same sex, and both have responded emotionally to that disruption.

The response in each case will affect their relationships with their peers as well. They may feel insecure with others of their sex, assuming that because their parents rejected them, others will do the same. Their identity—specifically their *gender* identity—might be shaken. Or they may retain a fantasy of having the perfect parent, an idealized parent they dream about and wish they could have as a parent or friend. Or they might simply feel unusually strong needs for bonding with the same sex, but because of their parent's perceived rejection, they avoid their peers to protect themselves from any further rejection.

As perception generates emotional response, so emotional response creates emotional needs. If these children suffer gender-identity disturbances, for example, they will keenly feel the need for a strong, accepting male or female to identify with. If they hold onto their fantasy of an ideal image, they'll feel the need to find and bond with someone who matches that image. And if they feel alienated from peers of the same sex they'll feel especially strong needs for attention and approval from the very ones they feel alienated from.

Emotional needs can and do sometimes become sexualized. That is, at some point they are linked with sexual desires, so the object of the emotional need also becomes the object of sexual desire.

Because I believe this pattern to hold true in so many cases, I consider homosexuality to be a *function* through which *sexualized emotional needs* are fulfilled. This fulfillment may come through homosexual desires, or fantasies, or activities. The function is still the same.

Let me explain this further by examining each stage of this pattern.

Perception of Early Relationships

Most theorists agree that, whatever the cause of homosexuality, its development begins in early childhood. Since a child's parents are the most significant people in his life, his perception of them and of his relationship with them will profoundly influence his emotional development.

Your home was the first place you learned about relationships, and the lessons you learned there have influenced, and still influence, the way you relate to everyone. I'm sure that's why God places such importance on the family, setting it apart as sacred and vital. Within our homes we learn about marriage, friendship, brotherhood, and intimacy. We learn from what we see and experience, and we assume that what we're learning at home will hold true throughout life.

The family unit is also the first place you learned about yourself. You learned how valuable you were or weren't from your family. You developed ideas about your "lovableness" from the responses you got at home. There you were taught, directly or indirectly, how important you, your feelings, and your opinions were and are.

That's because, as a child, you naturally assumed that your parents were "godlike"—all-powerful, all-wise, and always right. After all, they were the big people, the ones in charge, and you were the dependent, limited child. So what they thought of you, you came to think of yourself. Your identity has been learned with the help of people who taught you, through your interactions with them, about yourself. Identity is not something we just come into on our own, outside influences shape our sense of who we are.

You can see this in the Genesis account of creation. Adam didn't just wake up one day and decide, "Oh, I guess I'm the first created human. Nice garden I've got here; I think I'll keep the place up. And that lovely lady must be my wife, so I'll mate with her and we'll populate the planet." No, he learned who he was, what was expected of him, and how much he was worth from *God*. It was God who taught him his purpose in life, and God who, though constant care and provision, gave him a sense of identity.

Christians are also subject to this. When we're converted, we begin to relearn our identity. Much of the Bible, especially the New Testament, teaches us who we are, why we are, and how important we are in God's sight. We, like Adam and the newborn child, learn our identity through another, higher source.

But we don't learn this exclusively through verbal teaching. It's not just our parents' *words* that we consider and take to heart; it is also their *responses* to us that teach us about ourselves. These are "messages"— nonverbal but clear communications between parent and child. They come in the form of a look, a touch, a tone of voice, even the amount of time they spend with us. Each of these sends us a message, not just about our parents but about ourselves. If a parent sends a child "affirming messages" through affection and attention, the child learns that he is safe and important because the parents say so. Likewise, when negative, hurtful messages are sent from parent to child, the child learns that he is not wanted, not valuable, unacceptable. Remember, the child has little confidence in his own insights, so he trusts his parents' judgment in these matters. "If Mom or Dad don't like me," he reasons, "then the problem is with me, not them. They know best; what they say goes." Remember too that the messages they send can be misinterpreted by the child.

An early perception of rejection or indifference from the parent of the same sex can be seen in the backgrounds of many homosexually oriented adults. In his book *Male Homosexuality* (Yale University Press, 1988) Dr. Richard Friedman cites 13 independent studies from 1959 to 1981 on the early family lives of homosexuals. Out of these 13, all but one concluded that, in the parent-child interactions of adult homosexuals, the subject's relationship with the parent of the same sex was unsatisfactory, ranging from a distant, nonintimate relationship to an outright hostile one. Most of them also indicated problems between the subjects and their parents of the opposite sex, but those problems were secondary in most cases.

These studies, by the way, were not conducted only with patients seeking professional help for their homosexuality. Studies by Evans (1969), Apperson and McAdoo

(1968), Snortum (1969), Thompson (1973), Stephan (1973), Saghir and Robins (1973), and Bell, Weinberg and Hammersmith (1981) were all performed with non-clinical subjects—people who were not undergoing psychotherapy and were not necessarily in distress over their homosexuality. Even these groups acknowledged that, early in life, something had gone wrong.

Friedman, who does not approach the subject of homosexuality from a Christian perspective and is in fact highly sympathetic to the gay rights movement, concludes:

> The weight of evidence discussed here seems therefore to implicate a pattern of family interactions in the development of homosexual men.[3]

Later he reiterates the point by saying:

> An emotionally secure, nontraumatic, warm and supportive pattern has not been documented to occur with any frequency in the backgrounds of homosexual men.[4]

As early as 1941 W.D. Fairbain presented similar ideas:

> Frustration of his desire to be loved and to have his love accepted is the greatest trauma that a child can experience. Where relationships with outer objects (i.e. parents) are unsatisfactory, we also encounter such phenomena as...homosexuality and [these] phenomena should be regarded as attempts to salvage natural emotional relationships which have broken down.[5]

Does this mean that a faulty relationship with parents creates homosexuality? Not necessarily. Many heterosexuals have come from families that were highly dysfunctional. Many boys have been raised by unloving and even cruel fathers whose mistreatment didn't cause their sons to turn to other men for sex. Many girls were brought up by disinterested mothers, yet these girls developed a normal sexual orientation. *Problems between parent and child do not necessarily cause homosexuality.* And yet the fact remains that these problems existed in the family backgrounds of most homosexually inclined adults. Why?

First, let's remember that sin manifests itself in any number of ways, yet sin is still the root problem. So a boy who is unloved by his father will develop some type of problem later in his life. Drugs, violent behavior, or antisocial tendencies might all be traced back to this root. Homosexuality is only one of many possible manifestations of poor family relationships.

But let me take this point even further. It was not what *actually happened* between you and your parents that contributed to your homosexuality. Instead, it was the way you *perceived* your relationship with them, and the way you emotionally *responded* to that perception. (This may explain why your sexual development took a different turn from your brother's or sister's. You responded in one way, they responded in another.)

"Perception" and "response" are the two key words here. In all relationships, we perceive the other party as having a certain attitude toward us, and we respond to the other party according to our own perception of their attitude. If we think somebody likes us, whether they really do or not, we'll feel comfortable with them and probably want their friendship. Likewise, if we perceive someone else as being unfriendly and rejecting, we'll tend to avoid them.

Haven't you seen this principle at work in your social life? Remember the times you've wanted to get to know someone, only to feel, because of the way he looked at you or because of his tone of voice, that he wanted nothing to do with you? No doubt you responded to your perception by saying, "Who needs him anyway?" or by feeling hurt and rejected. Later you may have found that you completely misunderstood him. You may have learned he was just in a bad mood when you met him, or that he's rather shy at first and doesn't warm up until he gets to know a person better. In those cases you found that your initial perception was wrong and that you had responded to a misconception.

Likewise in your early years you may have had parents who loved and highly valued you, but for some reason the communication of that love got blurred. You may have perceived your father to be disinterested in you, when in fact he cared very much about every part of your life. Still, you didn't respond emotionally to what really was—only to what you *thought* was reality.

In both cases, whether your same-sex parent actually rejected you or whether you simply perceived that rejection, you responded emotionally to what you saw or perceived. And that emotional response was probably the beginning of strong, unfulfilled needs contributing to erotic same-sex attractions.

Emotional Responses to Early Perceptions

The response to an early perception of rejection may take three forms, all of which can contribute to homosexuality: Problems of Gender Identity, an Idealized Image, or Same-Sex Deficits.

1. *Problems of gender identity.* Your gender identity is your basic sense or perception of your mascuinity or femininity. Money and Ehrhardt describe it as "the private experience of gender role, and gender role is the public expression of gender identity." Your gender role is the role your culture expects you to play as a man or

woman, so of course it varies from culture to culture. Your gender identity is determined by your confidence in that role. Since our society places a high premium on gender roles, your ability or inability to fulfill them seriously affects your general well-being.

Gender Identity Disorder is a clinical term describing a serious conflict between a person's *assigned* gender (male or female) and his *desired* gender. This disorder may show itself in transsexualism, or the desire of a man to actually be a woman, and vice versa. But Gender Identity Disorder is a far cry from homosexuality, and it is not commonly found among homosexually oriented adults.

But Dr. Friedman points out that feelings of being *unmasculine* or *unfeminine* are common among such adults. He proposes that unmasculinity, for example, is not necessarily femininity, but a lack of confidence in a boy's/man's own ability to fulfill the masculine role. This unmasculine or unfeminine experience, which I consider to be a *problem of gender identity* rather than a *Gender Identity Disorder*, has been noted by a number of investigators. Ten studies cited by Friedman, conducted between 1962 and 1984, have turned up the same results: a link between problems of gender identity and adult homosexuality (Friedman, 1988).

For example, in 1981 Bell, Weinberg and Hammersmith interviewed 979 homosexual men and 477 heterosexual men to determine which developmental ingredients may effect sexual orientation. Among their findings was evidence that "gender nonconformity" (their term) was closely linked to homosexuality:

> Even among non-effeminate homosexual men this Dislike of Boys Activities is the strongest predictor of Adult Homosexuality. While their nonconformity may not have been so obvious either when they were growing up

or in adulthood, it would appear that where they thought they stood on a masculine-feminine continuum when they were young was predictive of their eventual sexual orientation (Bell, Weinberg, and Hammersmith, *Sexual Preference: It's Development in Men and Women,* 1981).

How does this problem of gender identity come about? Like homosexuality, it is not inborn, but acquired through interactions, perceptions, and responses. A secure masculine or feminine identity usually develops through bonding with an older figure of the same sex, usually the father or mother, and emulating that older figure.

A few years back a delightful Australian film titled *The Bear* came out in American theaters. In it a young grizzly cub, orphaned after his parents were shot by hunters, tries to bond with an older grizzly, who at first wants nothing to do with him. But the cub shows remarkable tenacity, trying to snuggle up to the older bear whenever he sees him, only to be rebuffed and swatted away. Finally, when the older grizzly is shot by those same hunters, the young cub wins his heart by licking the gunshot wounds the grizzly is unable to reach. The two bond, and throughout the film the cub develops more "adult grizzly" characteristics by identifying with his surrogate father.

The film provides a pretty good model of gender identity development. When the father/mother figure is willing to bond with the child of the same sex, this invites the child to emulate and identify with the parent. The child will be inclined toward this process, desiring it intensely, but avoiding it if he feels unwelcomed or unaccepted by the parent.

Should that avoidance occur, it can be the beginning of gender identity problems. As mentioned earlier, the child views the parent as "right"; that is, if the parent seems to reject the child, the child assumes it's his fault, not the parent's. This can undermine a child's confidence not only as a *person*, but as a *boy* or *girl*. Problems of gender identity, then, begin with the child's belief that he is unacceptable to the parent of his sex, and therefore unacceptable to all members of his sex. This robs him of confidence to fulfill his gender role, having felt no invitation to emulate and identify with his father or her mother, leading to acute feelings of *unmasculinity* or *unfemininity*.

These feelings are confirmed during later development. After all, confidence with peers is largely determined by confidence at home. So if a boy feels ill-equipped to deal with other boys through traditional masculine activities, he'll be inclined to avoid those activities, which disrupts his ability to bond with other boys, which reinforces his belief that he is unmasculine.

Case in Point: Gerard

Gerard remembers his earliest years as pleasant ones during which he related freely to both parents, though he felt mildly intimidated by his father, who was a machinist—rugged, tall, and noticeably masculine. One unfortunate incident triggered a series of events that would shape his sexual development. During a particularly heated argument with his mother that was taking place in Gerard's presence, his father picked him up and threw him across the room. While he cowered in the corner, the fight ensued for another hour or so, followed by a tense silence. When it was all over, the whole family gathered together and watched television as though nothing had happened. Gerard was five at the time, and couldn't comprehend what had happened. Nor could he understand his father's silence—no apology, no explanation. He concluded (wrongly) that Dad disliked him. Gerard began to withdraw from the man, preferring the company of his mother, who seemed safer and more predictable.

His withdrawal didn't go unnoticed by his father, who apparently didn't understand Gerard's reasons for avoiding him. This only enraged him, causing him to resent what he perceived as Gerard's rejection of *him*. He began criticizing the boy, taunting him with labels like "sissy" and "Mommy's little girl." Gerard, of course, responded by retreating further from his father and assuming that he was indeed more acceptable to girls than to boys. With that perception of himself, he entered elementary school believing he should play with the girls, which reinforced his gender identity problems and caused other boys to likewise consider him a sissy. The label stuck (even though there was nothing noticeably feminine about Gerard) and he went through his first 23 years of life convinced he was decidedly unmasculine.

2. *Idealized image.* It's not uncommon for children to idealize their parents; in fact, it's uncommon for them not to. After all, a Daddy looks pretty big and powerful to a little boy, and a Mommy looks beautiful and competent to a little girl. Children naturally want to be like their same-sex parent, at least for a time. They see them as powerful, wise, and ideal.

Normal development allows for a gradual disappointment in our parents. If you're a parent you know that, sooner or later, you're going to blow it. You can't possibly be the perfect Mom or Dad your kids want you to be, and so eventually, to some degree, they'll be disappointed in you just as, to some degree, you've been disappointed in your own parents.

That's actually good for us, because through disappointment we become more realistic and mature. We learn through this disappointment to accept people's limitations. And so a child's ideal image of his father or mother gradually changes to a more realistic viewpoint. As he grows, he's able to see his parents' imperfections, but since he's growing emotionally as well as physically, he can handle the knowledge that they're not perfect. That's basic process: As we grow, biologically and emotionally, we learn to accept hard realities like death, injustice, and our parents' imperfections. The more we mature, the better able we are to let go of our early idealism.

At times, though, this process is aborted by early trauma. If a child is shocked by a sudden rejection from a parent, or a parent's early disappearance, he might not have the capacity to handle the loss. Instead of gradually relinquishing the ideal image he had of his father, he may cling to it, hoping to someday find it again in somebody else.

Case in Point: Alan

Alan's early tragedy is a good example. He had seen little of his father during the first three years of his life. He and his sister were raised by his mother while his dad worked a graveyard shift. Alan vaguely remembers the few times he had been alone with Dad, times during which he felt Daddy was the most wonderful person in the world. He saw his father as a remote, godlike figure whom he could occasionally get a glimpse of. But unknown to him, his father was having severe episodes of depression, and had been undergoing intensive therapy.

Shortly before his third birthday, Alan's father called him into the kitchen. He sat him down at the table, smiling strangely and saying "Watch this." He then poured himself a glass of wine mixed with chemicals, gulped it down, and passed out. Within minutes, he died as Alan watched in confused horror.

The shock was too much for the three-year-old boy. Rather than face the full weight of what had happened, he retained the idealized image he had had of his father. It provided him with comfort during the following years, and throughout his life he looked for this image to show itself in other men. It finally did, in the form of a man who propositioned Alan and initiated his first homosexual encounter. Though he was well into his fifties at the time, his need for a wonderful man to take care of him expressed the longings of an unfulfilled child.

3. *Same-sex deficits.* There is a period of life, usually between early childhood and pre-adolescence, during which we almost exclusively seek out members of our own sex. Boys cluster with boys, and girls cling to each other. Sometimes kids express an almost-lighthearted contempt for each other. Little boys think girls are "weird"; the girls think the little boys have "cooties." That's normal, even necessary. Our identity as male or female is solidified when we bond with our own gender. Only when our need for bonding with the same sex has been fulfilled can we move on to relationships with the opposite sex.

During this period I believe there are three kinds of relationships with our own sex that we especially need: a nurturer, a mentor, and a comrade.

Our same-sex nurturer will usually be our parent of the same sex. This parent welcomes us to bond with him, making us feel comfortable and accepted in his presence. Our relationship with him is marked by physical affection, play, and intimate caring. He delights in us, giving us a sense of "specialness." As we become secure in his love, we develop an early conviction that we're "O.K." as males or females, perfectly acceptable and lovable to our same-sex nurturer and therefore to other members of our sex.

Our same-sex mentor may also be a parent, or perhaps an instructor, coach, music teacher, older child, or any adult figure who takes a special interest in us.

Through our mentor we are gradually initiated into our gender role. No matter what technical role our mentor plays (teacher, coach, big brother, etc.) our relationship with him increases our confidence with members of our sex outside of our family. His relationship is less nurturing and more instructional. He expects more out of us than our nurturer, and challenges us to further develop our masculinity. He provides us with a sort of "rite of passage."

Same-sex comrades are vital to a healthy personality. Our comrades mirror us, compete with us, bond with us, and make us feel like "one of the guys/girls." We grow with them, sharing our experiences of school, puberty, dating, social struggles, and so forth. They stabilize us. And our relationship with comrades spurs us on, because we inevitably compare ourselves to them, creating a healthy competition. Through our comrades we learn to feel good about ourselves and comfortable with our own sex.

If we lack any or all of these relationships, we develop what Psychologist Dr. Elizabeth Moberly calls "same-sex deficits." In her book *Homosexuality: A New Christian Ethic* she stresses the importance of same-sex love between parent and child, and theorizes that the homosexual urge is an attempt to make up for deficiencies in the early father-son, mother-daughter relationship. Because of those deficiencies, a child may feel that the normal avenues for same-sex love (nurturing, mentoring, comradery) are not available to him. He thinks, because of parental rejections, that he is not qualified to engage in normal friendships with his peers. This prohibits the very thing he needs the most—love from and closeness to members of the same sex. He wants it so badly, yet he feels that if he tries to get it he'll experience further rejection. This leaves him in a quandary: same-sex intimacy has become the thing he wants the most, yet he avoids the normal activities that provide it because he feels as though any attempts to participate in those activities will fail, leaving him lonely and in pain.

He responds with what Moberly calls "Defensive Detachment." He detaches himself from his peers and parent of the same sex, because attempting to relate to them causes him pain. Although such relating could be the source of healing for him, he sees it as threatening, avoiding it because he refuses to re-experience the hurt he is sure will come. He may comfort himself with isolation, or by devaluing father and peers ("They're jerks anyway—who needs them?"), often rejecting the very masculinity they symbolize. In a way, this protective device works well. By taking no chances, he avoids further rejection. At least he remains emotionally safe.

But his "safety zone" of isolation doesn't kill his ever-deepening need for intimacy. In fact, the more he isolates himself, the stronger that need grows. This is not homosexuality, mind you; rather, it is the legitimate, normal need for bonding that all of us have experienced. In this case, though, the need has grown and remained unsatisfied.

Case in Point: Martin

Martin's father never overtly rejected him. In fact, Martin recalls no specific mistreatment at his father's hands. He worked hard and provided well for his family, but his marriage suffered. His wife longed for more attention than she was getting from him (he was reserved, not given to the affectionate expressions she craved), and he resented her requests for more of his time and attention. She responded by withdrawing from her husband and focusing her needs for affection on her son.

Martin was to be a sensitive, intelligent child who provided a listening ear and sympathetic support to his mother, who began confiding in him as she would to a close friend. Confidant, friend, and comforter, Martin learned that his prime function in the home was to "take care of Mom," whose needs were growing as her marriage deteriorated. She began drinking heavily, and Martin began covering up for her and becoming her caretaker. His father, meanwhile, came to resent the bond that mother and son shared, and accordingly withdrew emotionally from both. This only strengthened Martin's conviction that he should stay close to Mom, who seemed to need him so badly. By early adolescence he had virtually no social life; he was too busy at home.

He missed out on all three relationships important to children. He had no male nurturer, no mentor, no comrade. He was by no means effeminate, but he retained a huge need for bonding with his own sex. At times he would fantasize about being in helpless, dangerous situations in which a strong male figure—a Superhero of sorts—would come along and rescue him, commending Martin for his bravery and consoling him. This fantasy expressed a desire for male nurturing and mentoring that would continue for years, a desire that was combined with a wish for the type of friendships he saw other boys enjoying. When he entered into his first homosexual relationship, Martin felt that he had finally found the nurturer, mentor and comrade he had been longing for all his life.

In each of these cases, certain emotional responses were influenced by the perceptions a child had of himself, his parents, and others of his sex. And these responses inevitably gave way to deep and unsatisfied needs. Emotional responses to early perceptions, whether they take the form of gender identity problems, idealized images, or same-sex deficits, leave a child with specific needs for intimacy with his own sex.

Sexualization of Emotional Needs

Sexual needs are natural to sexual beings. They are the result of the biological drive and the human need for romantic intimacy. There is nothing unhealthy or unusual about them. *Sexualized needs*, however, run a different course. These emotional needs that are expressed indirectly through sexual activity, acted out through a sort of sexual pantomime. The needs themselves are usually legitimate, but the vehicle used to express them is not. We can see several examples of sexualized emotional needs in everyday life. Plenty of men use sex as a means of reassuring themselves that they're virile, competent, masculine. They delight in sexually conquering women, then bragging about their conquests to other men, causing them to feel manly and complete. Of course, their desire for confidence is a legitimate, understandable one. But sexually exploiting women is an illegitimate means of satisfying that desire. Likewise, many women are promiscuous not because they are sex-starved, but because during sex they're made to feel special and cared for. Again, their needs are perfectly normal, but their method of satisfying those needs is immoral, even dangerous.

This is true of other emotional needs that people express indirectly. Some people, for example, try meeting their need for comfort through food, gorging themselves whenever they're depressed or angry. The use of food has become their emotional outlet, and eating disorders may result. Others sexualize objects rather than people, finding erotic excitement through fetishes (shoes, leather items, etc.). No one can say exactly why people prefer those methods. All that can be said is that somewhere along the line they found a combination of emotional and sexual fulfillment through unnatural means. What they're seeking—comfort, peace of mind, sexual pleasure—is not wrong in and of itself. It's the way they're seeking it that is unnatural.

Exactly how, and under what circumstances, do these needs become sexualized? Why are they sexualized in some people but not in others? No one can say for sure. We do know that erotic feelings provide some of our earliest experiences of pleasure. Infants and children explore their bodies, lingering over the body parts that feel especially good. This gives them a sense of warmth and comfort, the "good" spots providing especially pleasurable sensations. I believe that we associate warm, positive feelings with sexual response long before we even know what sex is, because we associate our sexual organs with pleasure and comfort.

It should be no surprise, then, that when a person longs for intimacy with another, that longing may include a desire to share sexual pleasure. For most people, that longing is directed toward members of the opposite sex. Normal development usually includes, as stated earlier, an early phase of bonding with the same sex. By the time this need for same-sex bonding has been satisfied, and the child is ready for relations with the opposite sex, he is also entering puberty with its accompanying sexual drives. Perfect timing! Right when we're emotionally prepared for romantic love, our bodies are following suit.

But what happens when we're not emotionally prepared for relationships with the opposite sex? What if, by the time we reach puberty, our need for same-sex love is still unsatisfied and predominant? Our bodies won't wait for our emotions to catch up. Instead, we may develop strong sexual desires which may cross, like wires, with our emotional needs. In that case, the emotional need for closeness and identification with others of our sex becomes a sexualized need, with members of our own sex being the object of both our sexual and emotional desires.

And so the emotional responses to early perceptions become sexual responses as well. The need for bonding and identifying with the same sex, accelerated by gender identity problems, becomes a sexual desire. The need to find an ideal male/female figure becomes a need to sexually merge with that figure. And the need for a nurturer, mentor, or comrade becomes a desire for sex with a nurturer, mentor, or comrade.

Back to our original question: Why you?

No one can say without really knowing both you and your background. But based on what we've seen thus far—some prevalent theories and the experiences of others like you—we can make some educated guesses.

It probably started with your perceptions. You began to see yourself as a child without resources. You know better than I exactly what resources you were lacking: affirmation, attention, a figure to identify with, or maybe a combination of all three. You couldn't articulate it back then; you only knew that something was missing. And that "something" probably centered around a need for a stronger bond with those of your own sex. Maybe you felt different from your peers, or alienated from one or both of your parents, most noticeably the one of your own gender. That hurt, no doubt. You wanted closeness; you felt distance. You can't really say, perhaps, who's to bless or who's to blame. Maybe there was obvious rejection from that parent, maybe not. But the result is the same either way: You weren't as close to that parent as you needed to be.

Maybe you responded by withdrawing, creating your own world of safety and fantasy. Or perhaps you simply waited for someone special to love you and take care of you. You may even have become angry, resolving to never again let yourself feel hurt or rejected by another member of your own sex. No matter, each of these responses affected your relationships with other boys/

girls and, eventually, other men and women. You felt different from them, too. They may never have known your feelings of "differentness," but you were all too aware of them. They persisted, giving rise to an aching desire to bond, to be close, to feel accepted.

At some point, perhaps very early, maybe later, you realized that this desire was more than emotional. It was accompanied by sexual longings. Most likely, you were aware of those longings before you even knew what homosexuality was. Then one day you heard the word "queer," "dyke," or "homosexual," pondered its meaning, put two and two together, and realized you were one of "them." It became your secret, most likely difficult to keep and even more difficult to bear. You didn't ask for these feelings, but you learned that they were unacceptable to most people. That didn't encourage you to talk them over with anyone, even those closest to you. Your secret became your private burden, one you carried for years.

Perhaps even to this day.

So for you, homosexuality, whether expressed through actions or fantasies, represents legitimate emotional needs that have not been satisfied through normal means. You're not mentally ill, reprobate, or retarded. In fact, you may be a highly capable adult who functions well in most areas. But at some point you've found deep satisfaction through homosexual relating.

Remember, homosexuality has served a function for you. Now's the time to do some serious, reflective thinking. What exactly has that function been? What kind of satisfaction have you found through your homosexual fantasies or actions? Only you can answer these questions. When you do, you'll know not only what you've been seeking, but what you still need. Count on it— giving up homosexual contacts won't kill the emotional needs that led to them in the first place. More than ever, you need to meet them, legitimately, as fully as possible.

Whatever answers you come up with, you can be sure that what you've been looking for is still available. There are still close relationships to be found, friendships to enjoy, and love and intimacy with the same sex and the opposite sex to be experienced. These are the birthrights of any human, and your hunger for them is God-ordained. They are the vehicles for the security and self-confidence that every child and adult seeks.

6

The Process of Change

The idea that homosexuality can be changed is nothing new. The apostle Paul referred to homosexuals when writing to the Corinthian church, then said, "And such *were* some of you" (1 Corinthians 6:11). We cannot believe the Bible without also believing that God redeems His people, forgiving them of sin and freeing them from its dominion over their lives. Homosexuality is no exception.

Although the Bible is authoritative, it's also nice to know that professional opinion has backed up its teaching in this area. Certainly there are mental health practitioners who contend that homosexuality is irreversible and is a normal variation of human sexuality that should be accepted, not changed. But they don't represent the entire profession.[1] So before we discuss the process of change, let's hear from some experts.

Some people do change their sexual orientation. There is absolutely no harm in trying.[2]

—Dr. John Money

Despite the rhetoric of homosexual activists, all studies which have attempted conversions from homosexuality to heterosexuality have had significant success.[3]

—Glenn Wood and
John Dietrich

I have recently had occasion to review the result of psychotherapy with homosexuals and been surprised by the findings—a considerable percentage of overt homosexuals became heterosexual.[4]

—Ruben Fine

No matter how much remains to be learned in this field, it is evident that people can and do recover from this neurosis. Some to a highly satisfactory extent, though not completely, some completely, by all accounts.[5]

—Gerard Van Den Aardweg

We have followed some patients for as long as ten years who have remained exclusively heterosexual.[6]

—Irving Bieber

I've heard of hundreds of other men who went from a homosexual to a heterosexual adjustment on their own.[7]

—Lawrence Hatterer

Each person has to decide where his or her own satisfaction lies; there is no one formula. If the foremost priority in one's life is his religious faith, then his personal happiness might come from conforming to that faith rather than from pursuing his sexual orientation. With human beings, truly anything is possible.[8]

—Patricia Hannigan

If you are motivated and willing to exercise patience and discipline, you have good reason to be optimistic about change.[9] Let me stress again, though, the need for realistic expectations. Change does not occur quickly. In fact, it happens so gradually that you may hardly notice it at first. And, as stated earlier, change occurs to different degrees among different people. Some claim complete conversion of sexual desires from homosexual to heterosexual. Others experience reduction, not absence, of homosexual attractions. Still others allow that, although they are no longer aroused by their own sex, they could backslide or regress to homosexual attractions. Don't compare your process to others, or expect your experience to be exactly like theirs. In this as in all aspects of life, you are unique.

While deferring to the professional opinions mentioned above, let me add some of my own observations about change.

People definitely can and do change. I think, believe, *know* that to be true. But when they change, it is more often by degrees than by complete transformation.

Alfred Kinsey introduced the concept of a continuum of human sexuality. While I disagree with some of the other conclusions he drew in his 1948 study of male sexuality,[10] I do think this concept of continuum is valuable and true. People experience sexual attractions to a certain degree of frequency and intensity on a five-point scale, as listed here:

0 – Exclusively heterosexual, no homosexual attractions.

1 – Predominantly heterosexual, incidental homosexual attractions.

2 – Predominantly heterosexual, more than incidental homosexual attractions.

3 – Equally heterosexual and homosexual attractions.

4 – Predominantly homosexual, more than incidental heterosexual attractions.

5 – Predominantly homosexual, incidental heterosexual attractions.

6 – Exclusively homosexual attractions.[11]

"Males do not represent two populations, heterosexual and homosexual," Kinsey said. "Not all things are black nor all things white."[12] That is exactly why I dislike the term "homosexual" when used as a noun. People are not really homosexual or heterosexual, as I see it, but they are people who have, to some degree, homosexual or heterosexual attractions, or a combination of each. In this sense homosexuality is best used as an adjective to describe feelings, not people.

If homosexual attractions exist to degrees, I believe they also change by degrees. So a person who rates a Kinsey 6 is not likely to jump right into Point 1 or 0 (though I can't deny the possibility) but will instead change more gradually, point to point. How far will he go? How long will it take? No one can say. But I'm convinced that his change will follow the principle of a continuum; that is, he will experience homosexual desires to a lesser degree. They will become less predominant, giving way to a higher degree of and potential for heterosexual desires. I put no limit on the degree to which this change takes place, but I insist that it is by degrees that it usually takes place.

Process

How then does change happen? I see it occur in a five-point process.

1. Homosexual behavior ceases.
2. Needs that have been satisfied through homosexuality are heightened and identified.
3. Nonsexual intimacy begins to satisfy identified needs.
4. Self-perception changes.
5. Sexualized emotional response to early perceptions changes.

1. *Homosexual behavior ceases.* This is necessary for two reasons. First, homosexual acts are sinful, and sin stunts emotional growth because it pollutes the entire personality. It increases guilt, weakens faith, and leads to depression (and often to despair). No one can successfully grow when willfully committing sexual sins.

Second, if homosexuality has served as a function to fulfill certain needs, it logically follows that, as long as a person continues to commit homosexual acts, then the needs they fulfill will be repressed. Viewed this way, homosexual behavior is like holding a basketball underwater. As long as the ball is held down, it won't come to the surface. When it's released, it will show itself. So it is with the emotional needs that lie behind homosexuality. They cannot be clearly identified as long as homosexual behavior holds them "underwater," beneath consciousness. And as long as they remain unidentified, they can't be recognized and legitimately fulfilled.

2. *Needs that have been satisfied through homosexuality are heightened and identified.* When the

basketball is released, it bobs to the surface and is easier than ever to identify. And when homosexual behavior is removed, the needs behind it become more acute than ever. That's why many people have such a difficult time abstaining from it. It's not just sexual temptation that draws them back, but the desire to satisfy these needs in the old, tried-and-true way. Some would say that few people really change because homosexuality is so deeply ingrained. I'm more inclined to think that many people give up at this point because they refuse to tolerate the frustration of feeling unsatisfied emotional needs. Like the children of Israel wandering in the desert, they long for their familiar past and the satisfaction it gave them.

> I never knew how hooked I was on sexual acting out until I gave it up. Since then I've felt more lonely and depressed than ever. It doesn't seem fair that I've given up something that's wrong but still feel all these conflicts. It just makes me want to go back. I don't really want to do it with a man again, I just want to stop the pain (male counselee).

Using the model of homosexual development I proposed in the last chapter, suppose a man's homosexual behavior satisfied his need for a nurturing male to take care of him. He turns away from this behavior, only to find that he needs such a nurturer more than ever. But the only way he's gotten that nurturing in the past is through homosexuality. He hasn't yet learned nonsexual ways of getting what he needs, so he goes through a season of waiting while the need continues to throb away. It almost seems cruel—"unfair," as my counselee said.

But that's exactly how legitimate needs are eventually satisfied! First they make themselves known. Only then can a person plan legitimate, nonsexual ways to satisfy them. Another counselee put it well:

> I thought I wanted sex. I still do, I guess, but more than that I want to feel special to somebody. I want to feel that a man really cares whether I live or die. I want to know that I have at least one person who's close to me and really accepts me as I am. And I want that person to be somebody who's "together," not just some loser who'll latch on to anybody. I want to feel honest-to-God accepted by a man I can look up to. In fact, I want to be like that man (male counselee).

3. *Nonsexual intimacy begins to satisfy identified needs.* The frustration of unmet needs motivates the Fighter to look for alternative, nonsexual ways to meet them. This often means conquering the Fighter's long-held fear of his own sex. When he confronts that fear by allowing himself nonsexual closeness with other men, he finds healing in that closeness. He begins to feel specialness, the security or affection he sought in homosexual relationships, and he learns that sex isn't the only way to obtain those feelings. This is when real healing begins—when a person receives through normal relationships the benefits he used to get through abnormal ones.

4. *Self-perception changes.* The early perceptions mentioned in Chapter 5 came about through early relationships. The child perceived his parent to have a certain attitude toward him ("Dad doesn't like me," "Dad thinks I'm unimportant") which he then internalized, or came to believe about himself ("I'm not likable," "I'm unimportant"). These are perceptions based on what the child assumed his parent thought

about him. When, as an adult, he allows other important figures to relate to him, he begins to internalize *their* thoughts toward him. ("This person values me as an equal, not a sexual partner or a subordinate. If he thinks I'm valuable, maybe I really am valuable!") That is the power of healthy friendship. It revolutionizes the way the Fighter sees himself, because it provides proof that someone else thinks he's worth spending time with and being close to. And when that closeness is nonsexual, it challenges his belief that sex is the primary way to feel same-sex closeness.

5. *Sexualized emotional response to early perceptions changes.* When a perception changes, the response has to follow suit. So if a person has perceived his own sex as being distant and inaccessible, he will respond with an intense longing for same-sex closeness. Likewise, if through normal friendships instead of homosexual relations he learns that his peers will love and accept him, his need for same-sex closeness will diminish. It will partially remain, of course, because to some degree we will always need to bond with members of our own sex. But the need for that bonding will be less intense.

Intimacy with our peers is like water; we always need it to a degree. But if we've gone without it for a long period, our need for it turns into a craving that will drive us to do almost anything to get it. We may even drink seawater or gutter water if our thirst is intense enough and we don't think there's any other way to satisfy it. When a strong emotional need has been sexualized, its satisfaction can be sought in a number of illegitimate ways, including homosexuality. But when that need is being met legitimately, homosexual behavior holds less appeal. That too is a sign of real change.

At this point there may still be homosexual attractions, even when the problems that originally created them are being resolved. Often these attractions have become learned responses to a certain stimulus, a kind of knee-jerk reaction. But when knee-jerk reactions are not reinforced through repetition, they diminish. If they have been learned, they can also be unlearned.

This process of change is dependent on relationships that are close and nonsexual. And so the process of the development of homosexuality and change comes full circle. The problem *started* in a relationship and is *resolved* through relationships. I can't overemphasize this point: All of the prayer, insight, and effort you can muster won't change your sexual desires one bit if you don't establish the kind of relationships you need. Homosexuality is an attempt to satisfy yourself through an unhealthy relationship. Now is the time to learn how to satisfy yourself through healthy ones!

7

Maintaining Sexual Integrity

Here's an unflattering thought to consider: Everything is in a constant state of decay. Without maintenance, things deteriorate. So do people. So will you. If you can accept that fact, you'll avoid the apathy that keeps some Fighters from maintaining their sexual integrity.

Not convinced? Look at your yard. It isn't naturally inclined toward beauty. It has beauty's potential, but to bring that potential out you have to keep it from doing what it's naturally inclined to do—grow weeds, dry out, die. How about your body? It's a great machine, but it's not naturally inclined to stay in shape. If you want to avoid obesity, scruffiness, or body odor, you have to work on it, exercising and grooming it daily. The same can be said of almost anything—pets, finances, houses. Without constant attention and maintenance, things naturally decay.

The gains you make toward sexual wholeness are also

subject to decay. Every new level of maturity you achieve will be challenged, because you live in a fallen world, one that is hardly sympathetic to your commitment to purity. That's one reason sexual temptations linger after repentance, no matter how earnest the repentance has been.

I'm not suggesting you go through life paranoid, or that you keep looking over your shoulder to catch an oncoming temptation before it catches you. I'm only warning you to guard your integrity.

A State of Consistency

Sexual integrity is a state of consistency, in which your sexual expressions are consistent with God's standards. It is, again, a question of stewardship. You have not repented of your sexual *nature,* which means you are still responsible to keep it under control and reserved for its proper use.

After repentance there is usually a period of real joy. Clear conscience, a sense of freedom, and newfound optimism make a powerful combination. You feel zealous, eager to make a new start. And when, through enlightenment, you learn about yourself and finally get answers to some long-held questions, that's doubly exciting. It frees you up, giving you that "Aha!" kind of feeling. ("Now I finally understand!") This phase is so energizing that many people mistake it for a complete deliverance from sexual temptations. "Now that I've given up my sin, and understand why I got involved with it in the first place, I know I could never go back," they say. On the one hand, that's a great attitude. It's a legitimate high. But it's also, sad to say, a temporary stage. Sooner or later temptations will come, and the rather mundane task of day-to-day maintenance replaces the understandable but unrealistic exhilaration.

This is nothing new. Jesus Himself said that many people receive the Word with great joy for a season, but if they have no root in themselves they fall away when tribulation comes. Not *if* it comes; *when* it comes! So the best defense against falling away is maintenance.

Sexual integrity is an act of the will, expressed through day-to-day decisions. It's really that simple. Whether you succeed or fail in this area will be determined by your willingness to make, and stick to, daily decisions to keep your sex life consistent with your standards. (Yes, you do have a sex life whether you're sexually active or not. As long as you have sexual desires, you have a sex life.)

It's also a matter of strategy. Integrity is maintained when you have a predetermined plan for dealing with the sexual temptations that you are most prone to. It's like gardening. To keep a yard up, you need to pay attention to maintenance, keeping the yard free of weeds, leaves, or any elements which prohibit healthy growth.

So even after making a new start, certain elements— weeds, of sorts—should be watched for and guarded against. Anyone who makes a major change has weeds to deal with: traces of old behavior, times of discouragement, and patterns to break. Fighters also have their special weeds. Common among these are compulsive sexual behavior, inner and homoerotic relationships.

Compulsive sexual behavior is no joke. It includes lust and poor self-control, of course, but it is much more than that. It is a repetitive, constant form of sexual activity that a person feels *compelled*—not just tempted—to indulge in. Usually this behavior is acted out in secretive, anonymous sexual encounters in parks, public bathrooms, or adult bookstores. Seldom does it include one lover; most often it means brief trysts with several partners, most of whom will never be seen again. Or it may be a solitary addiction to pornography. Regardless, it's a bondage of the worst kind because there's so much shame and remorse attached to it, making it terribly secretive and usually dangerous. It leads to arrest, broken marriages, and untold humiliation. If you've been hooked into it, you know that repentance alone won't stop it, although repentance is necessary. You've tried to stop before, I'm sure. Now that you're addressing the whole spectrum of your homosexual experiences, you're no doubt as serious as ever about breaking free. For that alone you deserve encouragement and wholehearted support. But you may feel reluctant to look for it, because secrecy, as well as compulsivity, is part of your problem.

Compulsive sexual behavior is highly secretive. When you are caught up in it, you're not prone to discuss it with anyone, so friends and family members seldom know what you're going through. It's a double life of sorts, involving a public image of normality versus a long-held secret. Usually the Compulsive Fighter discovers his "drug" relatively early in life, becomes dependent on it, and incorporates it into his behavioral makeup. If that's true of you, you're carrying a heavy load. You haven't felt good about your behavior or yourself, but have had no idea how to change. What you *do* know how to do is hide, and at that I'll bet you're a pro. The years of secret-keeping, excuses for prolonged absences from job and family while you're having sex, and lying to cover your tracks have taught you to conceal your actions and feelings. Besides the destructiveness of your actions, then, you suffered from an unwillingness to let anyone in.

Even if you've stopped—repented of this behavior—you should realize by now the cycles addictions can go through. I won't presume to say your repentance does no good, or that you're inevitably going to fall into your old patterns again. I'll only say that addicts of any kind should get help, because the problems that led to their addiction, just like the problems that lead to homosexuality, need to be settled before the condition will lose its power. "Just Say No" is a great start. But more needs to be done.

Let someone in immediately. You've developed a private world centered around your addiction, and the privacy is what's keeping it intact. Disrupt the privacy of your world, then, and you weaken both it and the addiction it protects. You'll be less inclined to repeat the behavior you've given up if you know someone else is involved in your struggle with you.

A trained Christian professional with experience treating addictions will be valuable to you. As always, you should get a referral from your pastor or a trusted friend if possible. But do find qualified help. With it, you can understand the roots of your addiction and build up the defenses against destructive actions that have been torn down over the years.

You also should get into a support group—a Christ-centered one—that's geared toward this problem. This provides you with a legitimate emotional outlet for the conflicting feelings you'll experience while you withdraw from your addition. And finally, get some accountability. To be accountable to someone means to let him in on your struggle and to keep him up on your progress. It's a giving over of your right to privacy to at least one person who has your permission to question you about your day-to-day activities and encourage you when you struggle. You may balk at this, thinking it's too oppressive, too childish. But don't kid yourself—you can't deal with sexually compulsive behavior by yourself. If you could, you'd have done so long ago.

Inward Pollution

Inward pollution is a much more common struggle— so common, in fact, that I'd say it's almost universal.

Your inner man is going to be attacked by two formidable challengers: erotic images and memories of past sexual encounters. Both of these are powerful opponents; both can be faced and conquered.

Erotic Images

I dare you to try to escape erotic images. There was a time you could do so pretty easily just by avoiding pornographic magazines, but those days are long gone. Take a drive and you'll see some model flashing his wares on a billboard. Thumb through a magazine—a *regular* magazine, mind you—and you'll get hit with clothing ads that show more flesh than clothes. Watch television and you won't get away from sexual themes no matter what channel you turn to. Try as you may, you can't get away from erotic images without going into hibernation. You're a prisoner in a cult of physical beauty, and the gods and goddesses of the Perfect Physique demand your attention wherever you are.

You probably respond to erotic images according to cycle: visual contact, stimulation, sexual arousal. You notice, or "flash on," a picture that got your attention, whether or not you wanted it to. There's a quick charge of stimulation, a recognition of the kind of image that excites you. You feel pulled into the image, prone to linger over it and consume it. Sexual arousal follows, with a drive to unite with the image in a mental sexual encounter.

You can abort this cycle through, again, simple decision-making. Go back to rule one: Integrity is a process of daily decisions to remain consistent with your beliefs. Nine times out of ten, you didn't decide to flash onto the magazine picture, billboard, or shirtless guy walking down the street. It was there, so you saw it. At the moment of recognition, though ("Wow, that's just my type"), you can decide to move on. The earlier you decide, the easier it is not to be obsessed with the image. Your responsibility is not to keep good-looking bodies out of your field of vision (an impossibility) or to force yourself not to be attracted by them. Rather, you're responsible to keep moving, not letting yourself dwell on what you are seeing.

Once you've torn your eyes away, though there's still the mental image of what you've seen and the sexual response that's already kicked into gear. Some call it "going into heat"—I guess that phrase will do. When you're in heat, you burn. It can't be helped. Your responsibility is to contain the burning, and yourself, by not letting it dictate to your body what it's going to do. ("My body belongs to me, I don't belong to it.") You grow considerably by doing this, because you exercise the emotional muscles of self-restraint and mental discipline. The payoffs are incredible.

Coming out on the winning side of a sexual temptation, though, is only part of what what you need to deal with when you're aroused by sexual images. The other dragon you have to fight is your own frustration.

Strugglers get so focused on being "cured" of homosexuality that they judge their entire well-being by the frequency and intensity of their same-sex attractions. "Not again!" they scream. "I can't believe that person turned me on. I'm so sick of this, how could those feelings still be there? I'm such a failure!"

The truth is, you're only a failure if you haven't done what you were able to do. Yours is not the responsibility of changing your feelings. You can't anyway; you should know that by know. Instead, you've got to concentrate on taking steps that will promote growth—correcting habits, setting relationships right, disciplining yourself to maintain your integrity—and let the growth come in its time. If it's slow in coming, that's not your fault. And beating yourself up over it will only frustrate the process. So instead of wringing your hands over your response to erotic images, I'd suggest you learn from them.

Yes, learn from them, because they could very well be a representation of the qualities you feel you lack, qualities which you should pursue and strengthen.

You may be surprised to hear that the images arousing you are only complementing an erotic image that was formed in your mind long ago. This image is an combination of people you've actually seen who made an impact on you, figures you've fantasized about, and bodily representations of concepts of masculinity or femininity that appeal to you. That's why certain "types" of people attract us. They remind us of our inner image— the bodily representation of characteristics that appeal to us.

Images are more like mirages than mirrors. Mirrors reflect what we are, while mirages represent what we need. (Thirsty man in the desert needs water, sees a mirage, you know the story.) Often we use these images in private fantasy to give us comfort, or heightened pleasure, or a sense of completion.

"No," you say. "I just use them to feel turned on." Okay, I'll buy that. But that "turned on" state is, I believe, another example of sexualized need. The images have a sexual quality, but they embody concepts we want to touch, or merge with emotionally. Our needs, at some point, have become sexualized and so the desire to emotionally bond with a certain "type" becomes a sexualized desire.

Case in Point: Larry

Larry's story provides a good example. The concepts of male strength held tremendous appeal to young Larry. He recalls his father as a kind but remarkably passive man, the son of a man who was similarly meek, quiet, and agreeable. His mother stood in sharp contrast. The world was her territory, and she knew it. She took charge of every situation, controlled all conversations, made all decisions, and unmercifully criticized those around her. Interestingly enough, Larry didn't so much resent her for this as her resented his father's allowing it. He felt that a man should be stronger than that, and longed for such a man to look up to and gain his own strength from.[1]

That man came to him, not in person but through a western film Larry saw when he was seven. In it, the hero showed himself to be everything Larry felt he, his father, and all men should be: strong, conquering, able to stand his ground against anyone. Larry was enthralled, idolizing this obviously exaggerated form of masculinity as boys often do. Midway through the movie, the hero whipped his shirt off, displaying the classic Hollywood he-man physique. Larry recalls no sexual feelings for the man at the time, but remembers deciding there was a direct link between a well-developed male body and all the concepts of masculinity he wanted to get close to and eventually have himself. The image stayed, became sexualized later, and gelled into homosexual desires. In this case, the image was a mirage, an unreal representation of what Larry felt he needed.

Dr. Moberly calls this "cannibalism," a concept she describes as a means of "consuming" a person (or image) sexually and thereby having the qualities he has, qualities which the "consumer" thinks he lacks. (Moberly, 1983). Erotic homosexual images can serve this purpose. They provide a concrete, bodily representation of qualities the Fighter thinks he lacks and unknowingly tries to obtain through a sexual merge. (Many of my clients, for example, have been especially attracted to a big brother or father image. Not coincidentally, their relationships with their fathers were unsatisfactory.)

I'm not advising you to stop and analyze pictures of good-looking men or women just to see what emotional needs you're trying to fulfill by sexually merging with them! But it is helpful to understand the reason these images have such appeal. When you do, you can begin working to adopt those qualities for yourself.

Erotic imagery needn't be blatantly sexual. The attraction to another person you see in day-to-day life can also be considered a struggle with imagery. Sometimes Fighters get especially discouraged by the attractions they feel for people they see. The "looking syndrome" has them baffled. "How can I ever stop looking at attractive people when they're all around me?" they moan.

First, let's make a distinction between looking and lusting. It's no sin to notice the fact that a person is good looking. Everyone does that, whether they admit it or not. I find that men are especially hung up about this, needlessly so. Most women feel quite free to openly admire another attractive woman. My wife, for example, will always spot a pretty woman in the room. She doesn't hesitate to comment on the other woman's hair, make-up, or figure. And she's certainly not lusting! So men, as well, do notice other attractive men. Noticing a man's good looks is no more perverted than noticing his new car or fancy suit. All it means is that your eyeballs are working.

You may, of course, be doing more "serious" looking than the man who has never had homosexual attractions. So the second question to ask yourself is this: Are you lusting after another man, or envying him? Are you comparing yourself to him to see how you match up? Believe it or not, that's what a lot of "cruising" is all about—comparisons. If that's the case, what exactly is it that you admire about him? His mannerisms? Physique? Features? Does he have something that you want for yourself? That's not necessarily bad, if it spurs you on to improve yourself in the areas that you can realistically improve on. (Some would argue that as Christians we shouldn't be overly concerned about our appearances. I'm not so sure. If improving your physique or grooming will feed your masculine confidence, I say go for it.)

Finally, if after ruling out the other possibilities you have to admit that you're simply lusting, don't wallow in it. Confess it to God and yourself, then move on. Don't beat yourself up over a simple, learned response to attractive people. I've come to believe that a Fighter's obsession with his attractions ("They're still there, darn it!") creates a bigger problem for him than the attractions themselves. What I've stated earlier bears repeating: It is no sin to be homosexually attracted. It only becomes a sin when you act upon or deliberately feed that attraction. It is up to God, not you, to diffuse those attractions, so don't take responsibility for what you cannot control. You've got enough responsibilities to contend with as it is.

Memories

Your past includes a whole repertoire of sexual fantasies and experiences. Though you've put those experiences behind you, you haven't, nor will you ever, banish them from your memory. They stay in your mind like an old movie, ready to be replayed and reviewed time and again. In a sense they're like a handy piece of pornography you can always pull out and browse through. They're not just passive, either. They won't wait for you to refer to them. They'll intrude into your thoughts like unwelcomed burglars, robbing you of a sound mind and clear thinking.

The past uses your memory to keep itself alive, attacking your integrity by reminding you how "good" it all was, or by condemning you with the memory of how bad it all was. Either way, old mental tapes are a constant nuisance to be dealt with.

Also, your past reminds you of a concrete way of dealing with loneliness, boredom, anger, or any number of negative feelings. It invites you to return to the old faithful method for getting temporary gratification, and you're especially susceptible to that invitation when you're not at your best. (Another good reason to be watchful.)

Assuming you've recently turned from homosexual activity, you're in a sort of Twilight Zone. That's neither bad nor good; it just is. You've given up a sexual function which made you feel complete, satisfied, beloved. It's a good thing you gave it up, of course. The problem is, you may not have found alternative methods—acceptable ones, that is—that will give you the same sense of satisfaction. So when you're hit with pressures, mood swings, or anxieties, your past urges you to go back to the coping mechanisms (homosexual activity) which have proven to be somewhat effective. Sinful, yes, but still effective. The allure of those effective methods also gnaws away at your integrity.

The good old days always look better in retrospect, especially when you're having Bad News Days. But isn't the fact that you're having struggles proof that you're stretching? Stretching isn't always fun. You stretch when you force yourself to try new behaviors, or when you deny yourself what you used to indulge in. When you stretch yourself, you exercise patience. And when stretching, you force yourself to go a little further than you've gone before. You get tired, so naturally your thoughts turn toward the days when you weren't stretching. Days you indulged. And, of course, your thoughts turn toward the indulgence itself.

Whether the past holds the memory of one particular lover, or of pleasureable times in general, it takes on an enchanting quality. It makes you feel your current life is empty, unsatisfying, and therefore fruitless.

Like the "heat" of arousal, these periods of looking back and longing for something different are usually cyclic. David had a similar experience when he envied the seemingly terrific lives of wicked people. "I was envious of the boastful, when I saw the prosperity of the wicked," he wrote in Psalm 73. Describing their strength and success, even when commiting evil deeds, he concluded, "I have cleansed my heart in vain, and washed my hands in innocence." (Translation: What good is godly living when the ungodly have it so much better? And what's the use in giving up ungodliness when it seems to provide more happiness than righteousness? Righteousness doesn't keep me warm at night!)

Then David looked ahead a little and considered not the good life the wicked enjoyed, but the end result of it. And it hit him like cold water: "Oh, how they are brought to desolation, as in a moment!" The value of right living, he concluded, is not its present satisfaction, though there is that as well, but its long range benefits.

And the value in leaving an ungodly though pleasurable past is that it has no future. Your memories look good only because you're not seeing them panoramically. Take them to their logical conclusion, considering not only what you did and enjoyed, but where it was leading you, and you get a more accurate picture of your past. That's how you shake off the power of "good" memories—you view them with an eternal perspective.

Then, of course, there's masturbation.

Don't look so shocked; of course we're going to talk about it. It's one of the earliest forms of sexual expression we experience, and the commonest form of sexual activity among humans. Yet it's the least discussed, most widely misunderstood, and most universally embarrassing sexual topic there is. So let's hit it head-on. Is it all right for you to masturbate?

First question: What does Scripture say? Nothing. Astounding, isn't it? After all, the Bible does not shy away from sexual discussion. In fact, by the time you've finished the book of Leviticus, you've read descriptions of bizarre sexual practices you probably hadn't even thought of before! Surely God knew that masturbation existed; I for one don't believe it's a twentieth-century invention. Yet the Bible is absolutely silent on the subject. (Some point to Onan's sin of spilling his seed on the ground during intercourse with his brother's widow, an act he was struck down for, as a prohibition against masturbation in Genesis 38:9. They're wrong. Onan was practicing a form of birth control to avoid impregnating his widowed sister-in-law.)

From the start, then, we have no biblical reason to say masturbation is automatically wrong. Christian authors such as Carlson (1983), White (1977) and Penner (1979) have come to the same conclusion. Lustful fantasies, however, are definitely wrong, and they usually accompany masturbation. In such cases, it is the fantasies, not the masturbation, that are biblically condemned. Otherwise, you can assume that the act itself violates no specific Scripture.

Second question. How do *you* feel about masturbation? Even though God doesn't necessarily prohibit it, if your own conscience is violated by it, it has become a sin for you. In Romans 14:23, when talking about Christian liberty, Paul said, "Whatever is not from faith is sin." In other words, if you don't personally believe a thing is right, you have to abstain from it whether it's biblically prohibited or not. So if you feel masturbation is wrong for you, the argument stops there. It's not an option.

Finally, does the activity rule you? Are you controlled by it, having to turn to it excessively as though it were a drug? Then you've been brought under the power of it. "All things are lawful for me, but I will not be brought under the power of any," Paul said (1 Corinthians 6:12). If you are consistently compelled to masturbate, then you have a problem. You're in bondage to something that isn't sinful in and of itself, but nonetheless has control over you. And that's a good enough reason to abstain from it.

Within these guidelines, you can make your own decision about masturbation. It's not necessarily wrong, nor is it always commendable. It depends on your conscience, and the power the activity has over you.

A Sound Defense

The best offense is a good defense. So battling inward pollution is best done by keeping the inner man clean, or spiritually minded. Paul illustrated the struggle between the flesh and the Spirit in Galatians 5:17 by calling it a war between the two. They do battle with each other incessantly, so that you never seem to keep your thoughts as clean as you'd like to. The trick is not to concentrate only on the negative (lustful thoughts) but to emphasize the positive. Paul's solution? "Walk in the Spirit, and you shall not fulfill the lust of the flesh" (Galatians 5:16). Practically speaking, that means a life of consistent inward prayer. To be in constant prayer doesn't mean living like a monk. Instead, it means a consistent awareness of God's presence, plus nonstop acknowledgment of His nearness to you and residence within you. It means instant confession of sin when it occurs, and a commitment to keep your thoughts centered on Him. Keeping the mind centered on God—His nearness, His goodness, and His unfailing love for you—is the best defense against mental impurity that I know of.

Pastor Chuck Smith of Calvary Chapel in Costa Mesa, California, used to describe the futility of merely trying to drive dark forces out of your life. He compared it to being in a darkened room. "When you're in the dark," he would say, "it won't do any good to walk around with a baseball bat trying to drive the darkness out. Instead, try turning on the light."

Walk in the Spirit—with the lights turned on—and inward pollution won't control you.

Homoerotic Attractions

Homoerotic relationships are distinct from homosexual ones in that they don't necessarily include sex, but they do include strong, mutual erotic attractions. And, unfortunately, they usually occur between Fighters. The reason is obvious: Two men with no history of homosexual attractions will probably not develop such attractions for each other, no matter how close they get. On occasion, a Fighter may experience strong attractions to a heterosexually inclined brother—a problem indeed, but different from that of two mutually attracted Fighters.

These situations—homoerotic entanglements—can arise when two men or women are part of a support group or specialized ministry dealing with homosexuality. They are drawn to each other, perhaps innocently at first, perhaps not. At times they are completely unaware of their attraction, only to find it cropping up in spite of their best intentions. At other times they've just been kidding themselves; they were sexually turned on to each other from the word "go" and pretended they were really just interested in brotherly love and support. In either case, the two are enmeshed in a sensitive, dangerous communion of desire and dependency. What began as a seemingly godly friendship has turned into a

snare. Should they consummate their lust, the repercussions are extreme.

It can happen to anybody. It does happen, in fact,
among people of all orientations. Pastors and therapists
fall into sexual relations with their counselees, church
members develop attractions for each other, sympathetic husbands become too involved with the problems
of another man's wife. An affair is seldom the original
plan; it gradually evolves when both parties refuse to
recognize the erotic longings growing between them.

So don't consider yourself immune to this. More to the
point, adopt this commandment: Thou Shalt Not Kid
Thyself. If and when you recognize strong attractions for
another Fighter, call them what they are. They're not a
special "Jonathan and David/Ruth and Naomi" kind of
love. They're not the beginning of a special friendship.
They are, in fact, erotic attractions that can lead you and
the other party to ruin. You know they're present when
you become mildly obsessed with another person, having to spend extra time with him at every support group
meeting or church service, needing to know he likes you
and wants your company. When you require a long hug
from him every time you say "hello," watch it. And if
you're thinking about him constantly during the week,
don't pretend there's no problem.

Instead, use common sense. You needn't flog yourself
over this situation; it's understandable though undesir-
able. But don't ignore it, either. Although there's not a
hard-and-fast rule for handling this, let me offer some
suggestions.

Don't assume you should admit your attraction to
another Fighter. Maybe you feel you should be honest,
but consider this: By disclosing your feelings to him, you
may well set up a stumbling block for him as well as
yourself. If he is likewise attracted to you, you might be
inflaming the very spark he wants to put out. I would
advise, instead, that you disclose this to your group

leader, pastor, or whoever you're accountable to. Ask for that person's honest counsel and let him be a part of your struggle through this.

Avoid having an exclusive relationship with the other Fighter. That only solidifies the problem. When you're together, include other people as well. Keep up your other friendships and you'll be less likely to invest all your affections in him.

And speaking of common sense, don't be foolish enough to spend time alone with a person you're attracted to, especially if you sense the attraction is mutual. That's not only wrong but just plain stupid. Draw clear boundaries, and stick to them. That's a part of the day-to-day decision-making that goes with sexual integrity—the decision not to do what you feel the most compelled to do at any given time.

Don't assume that a homoerotic relationship will last forever. If the two of you are sincere, and act on your sincerity, the attractions will diminish. Most likely they are idealizations, unrealistic and temporary, which will fade in time. Explore your response to this person with your counselor or pastor, and you might find it springs from an emptiness of your own which you're trying to fill with the erotic love of another Fighter. And so this relationship may actually become beneficial to you if it indicates an area of yours that requires attention.

In the Event of Emergency

Hopefully you'll maintain your integrity in the face of temptation. But there's the possibility that, in a time of stress or weakness, you'll fail. In that case, what happens when the runner stumbles?

If he's smart, he'll get back on the track ASAP.

You may stumble. It's a pretty serious thing to do, and there's no justification for it. You don't have to fall, and unless you were forcibly abducted, you certainly had the ability to say no to a sexual invitation. But should it happen, remember that your main goal, like the runner's, is to get back into the race.

Avoid the equally futile extremes of ignoring a sexual fall or wallowing in guilt over it. To ignore a sin is to pretend it's no sin at all, and you only deceive yourself with that approach. Until it's acknowledged, it can't be dealt with, and until it's dealt with, it can't be left behind. Wallowing in guilt over a fall is just as useless. Years of self-reproach won't undo a scrap of the damage, so put the whip away. Full atonement for sin was made at the cross—do you really think you can do better than that?

Instead, confess it immediately. That's how you're cleansed and forgiven. Confession to God is an acknowledgement that you've offended Him, as well as an admission of your inability to undo the wrong. The moment confession is made, fellowship with God is restored. Jesus wasn't kidding, after all, when He said that anyone who comes to Him will in no wise be cast out.

Integrity—the decision to remain consistent with your standards (and God's)—is made up of hundreds of small, moment-to-moment decisions. And each decision, when followed through, strengthens you to make another one. Success breeds success. And what is it you're trying to succeed at?

You're trying, and learning, to be governed by your convictions instead of your feelings. *That is the ultimate goal of maintaining sexual integrity.* Mankind was created to enjoy his passions, never to be ruled by them. So each decision to act out of conviction feeds your sense of integrity and, by extension, your freedom to follow your convictions. Self-respect, an important quality for anyone, is built up by maintaining your integrity. So in the end, ironically, the maintenance of sexual integrity, though it appears to be self-denial, is in fact self-fulfilling. Permanently, deeply so.

God's commandments were given not to restrict our lives but to make them free in the truest sense of all.

PART FOUR

The Struggle to Change

8

The Courage to Confront

God intervenes in people's lives by confronting the alienation that exists between them. His loving confrontation makes a person aware of his need for redemption and causes him to receive forgiveness through Christ, and so the restoration of a relationship between Creator and creation begins.

But it never stops there. God is also committed to reconciliation *between man and man*. The second commandment, "Thou shalt love thy neighbor as thyself," can't be fulfilled as long as human relationships are dysfunctional. It's the breach in human relationships that creates emotional problems, and it's the correcting of that breach that resolves emotional problems.

Trees don't cause you emotional pain; other *people* do. Faulty human relationships affect the soul in all its aspects, sexuality included. And so the healing of relationships promotes the healing of your sexuality. Healthy, appropriate relationships generate sexual wholeness, just as unhealthy relationships create sexual problems. So unhealthy relationships need to be confronted and corrected if real healing is to occur.

You accomplish this by addressing unfinished business in existing relationships, and then by correcting established but unhealthy patterns of relating to people in general.

Unfinished Business

Unfinished business is made up of all the things we would rather ignore: the argument that was never settled, the wrongdoing that was never addressed, the resentment that you've felt over something another person has done and still does. It's the question you never asked ("Why did you do this to me?") or the observation you held in and brooded over ("What you're doing is wrong, and it bothers me") because you felt it wasn't worth the trouble to say it. Better not to rock the boat. It seems more Christian, too, because we're supposed to forgive and forget, aren't we?

How easily we use Christianity as a justification for emotional cowardliness! Instead of airing our grievances like mature adults, we would rather "make nice" and silently resent, rather than confront, another person's wrongdoing. Compounding the felony, we tell ourselves that God would have it so, that to be Christ-like means to suppress all negative responses to another person, even when those responses are justified. Instead of honest, loving confrontation, we prefer avoidance, all in the name of godly love.

Yet God's love for us had no avoidance in it. He was ready to forgive, of course, but forgiveness couldn't be extended to us until we admitted our sin and asked for grace. Far from just granting a sort of amnesty to mankind, He sent His Son to be punished for our sins, demanding atonement before forgiveness, then required a recognition from us of our offenses, a recognition leading us to Christ and to reconciliation with the Father. Jesus taught the same principle of forgiveness between humans. In Luke 17:3 He said, "If your brother sins against you, rebuke Him." He didn't say, "If your brother sins against you, ignore it and keep smiling." He knows us. He knows that when we're wronged, we resent it. And He doesn't criticize that resentment; instead, He recognizes it and tells us to take the proper actions so it can be alleviated.

That's exactly why you need to first confront the unfinished business between you and the people who are significant to you. I may be presuming too much here. It's possible that your current relationships are satisfactory, healthy, and without unaddressed problems. But I have yet to work with a Struggler who doesn't suffer from unfinished business. That's because the roots of homosexuality can be traced to unhealthy patterns of relating, patterns which are carried into the present. And I've found, without exception, that when the Struggler fulfills his responsibility to abstain from homosexual actions and is ready to look at the nonsexual parts of his life needing correction, unfinished business with others invariably shows up.

Earlier we looked at problems between parent and child, and how they affect future relationships, both sexual and nonsexual. We allowed that a child's perception, rather than a parent's actions, can create these problems, so parents are not always to blame.

The point is worth repeating because parent-bashing is in vogue again. At different times it has been fashionable to blame parents for society's ills, citing their deficiencies as the culprit behind immoral or even criminal behavior. Psychology has certainly encouraged this at times by placing too much emphasis on past errors and too little on current responsibility. Today more than ever, we hear about the dysfunctional family and the awful things it's done to us. I think the term is widely overused, so much so that its original meaning is lost. After all, as long as any family is imperfect it can be called "dysfunctional," making all of us victims of a dysfunctional home. Originally, though, the term referred to a high degree of dysfunction (acute denial, abuse, emotional battering) and not just its technical presence. So the fact that our parents were imperfect hardly entitles us to accuse them of creating a dysfunctional home.

Still, there are times that parental behavior has been so seriously damaging that it needs to be confronted. Sexual abuse or child-battering, for example, are acts so destructive that the adult who suffered them as a child does carry scars and pain. That pain continues to cripple his ability to enjoy loving, trusting relations. And confronting the people who inflicted that pain on him will probably be necessary.

Less serious but also requiring attention are unhealthy patterns of relating between parent and child that continue into the present. Larry's case is a good example. The power that his mother exerted over the family continued well into Larry's adulthood. She still felt perfectly entitled to scrutinize any part of Larry's life, although he was nearly 40 years old. Without hesitation she would remark on his choice of friends, his religious beliefs, or his personal habits as though he was just dying for her opinion. Larry felt emasculated whenever he saw her. Family gatherings made him apprehensive because he knew what was coming.

In his case, his mother's dominance wasn't just a nuisance; it actually hindered his growth. In fact, the most noticeable homosexual temptations he experienced would occur right after a visit with Mom. Each encounter with her heightened his sense of need for a strong male figure to bond with, giving back to Larry a bit of the manhood his mother had lopped off. As long as he refused to confront the situation, he couldn't make progress. When he finally got angry enough to insist on a new way of relating, his homosexual fantasies diminished.

Your problems may not be with your parents. They may be with close friends, your spouse, or co-workers. But the principle is the same: As long as you allow unhealthy patterns to continue between you and the people most important to you, you will stunt your own growth.

Confronting Your Passivity

To correct a relationship's unhealthy patterns, you first need to confront your own reluctance to do so. Passivity is common among Strugglers. (Over 70 percent of my clients have exhibited noticeably passive behavior.) I see a direct link between the development of passivity and the early patterns leading to homosexual development. Both are caused by a child's perception and response.

Passivity—the inclination to avoid directness and allow unwanted behavior to continue—doesn't just happen; it's learned. And it's learned through early interactions, then reinforced in adulthood, as this model illustrates.

Early strivings
get an
inappropriate response,
so the child
protests
but is
invalidated,
which gives the child a
conviction of non-entitlement.

Every child strives toward his parents, seeking an appropriate response. The striving is an emotional drive for affection and reassurance from the parent, so the appropriate response, of course, is to give what the child is seeking. Most parents do.

But when an inappropriate response comes instead, the child reacts. If he sought attention and got ignored instead, or tried to give affection and was rebuffed, he will protest by crying, complaining, or pleading with the parent. If the parent responds by invalidating the child's protest ("Shut up or I'll really give you something to complain about!") the child develops a serious and deep conviction on non-entitlement:

"I'm not entitled to complain about anything, I guess. If I'm hurt or angry, nobody's going to care. And I'm not about to risk the humiliation of expressing my hurt, only to be told I've got no right to even be hurt!"

This conviction translates easily into passivity, making it look like the only option. If that's your situation, you probably allow people to speak to you pretty much the way they want to. Your boundaries aren't well defined; neither you nor others know just how much you'll take before you fight back. You ask for little, although others probably expect much from you. And, most of all, you're quite comfortable with your passivity. Like Lot reclining in Sodom, you've gotten used to the ways things are, even though you don't really like it, and you feel there's little you can do about it.

Start Now

But you've got to do something about it, and you've got to start now. Until you outgrow your passivity, you won't correct the problems between you and others which are stunting your growth. And unless you correct those problems, you'll never begin to enjoy the healthy, mutually beneficial kinds of relationships that will make you whole.

To confront unfinished business or correct current problems, you start by verbalizing your complaint. Not accusing or shouting, but verbalizing. You'll be surprised at what that can accomplish.

You see, relationships are like a set of gears which are interconnected. They fit together to form a system, a way of functioning. If you're passive, your gears are shaped one way. The people you relate to are shaped another, complementary way, and so your relationship runs like a set of well-fitted gears. You're passive, they exploit your passivity, and everything goes smoothly. Now you need to throw a monkey wrench between the gears, shaking the system up by serving notice that you are no longer going to allow certain things, and that you're acquiring a new set of boundaries and expectations.

So, for example, if your friends or family members are used to telling you what to do, you can shake the system up as follows:

"Joe, it's time you changed jobs. You're not making enough money where you work and I don't think you've chosen the right career anyway. After you quit your job, go back to school for a couple of years and get into another line."

"Al, I don't tell you where to work. When I want to change jobs I'll do so, not until then."

A simple statement from Joe to Al challenged the system. Al is accustomed to telling Joe what he should do, and is going to be surprised by Joe's response:

"Hey, I only want what's best for you! Why are you fighting me?"

"I don't tell you where to work and I'm asking you to show me the same respect."

Notice that Joe is not getting aggressive, nor is he backing down. He is quietly throwing a monkey wrench between the gears by letting Al know that he requires more respect than he's gotten in the past.

Also, you'll notice that Al is not exactly applauding Joe for his efforts. He's resisting, as people always do, Joe's new behavior. He'll probably challenge it:

"Joe, you've always been so nice. What's gotten into you?"

"I know I've let you boss me around. That's my fault as much as yours. But it needs to stop. I'll make my decisions, and if I want your advice you'll be the first to know."

Here's an important point: *You've got to take responsibility for the part you've played in your relationships.* What you've allowed, you're responsible for.

Also, you can't change people's expectations of you overnight. When they're used to treating you in a certain way, they won't want to stop. This isn't necessarily some sort of viciousness on their part; they, like you, have gotten used to your passivity. They don't like seeing the system changed, so they resist. That's O.K. As long as you're consistent and stand your ground, those around you will either learn to respect your new expectations, or they'll withdraw from you. (Sad but true, you may lose some friends when you decide to confront your passivity. People often like you better when you're unhealthy. But if someone prefers you to stay unhealthy, is his friendship really worth having?)

The importance of this conversation between Joe and Al is twofold: First, of course, it's the beginning of the correction of a long-standing problem—Al's dominance over Joe. Second, it is actually strengthening Joe's resolve to outgrow his passivity. Every time Joe responds to Al assertively, he reinforces his new behavior. He gains more confidence with each answer, and, when Al begins responding to Joe differently, Joe begins to see himself differently.

Success in Action

Success breeds success. Each time you verbalize your dissatisfaction with unhealthy patterns, you send a signal to other people that you're changing, and that the nature of your relationship with them will have to change if it's going to continue. While you're learning a new and better way to relate, you're retraining them as well, requiring more respect and appropriate treatment.

And so you draw the courage to confront people when you see the harm that unhealthy relationships have been causing you. You learn to correct these, and in so doing you come to see yourself as entitled to fairness and mutuality. In so doing you become stronger, though not tyrannical.

I warn you, though, you will feel tyrannical at first. New behavior feels odd, and if you're used to putting up with mistreatment, you actually feel like an ogre when you insist on something better. You'll feel guilty, even though you know there's no reason to. Don't let that stop you. Let your mind, not your emotions, dictate your actions.

Confronting your current relationship problems is the first step toward developing a new self-perception that will, in time, change your sexualized emotional responses. Developing new relationships is the next step.

9

Integration and Male Gender Identity

The link between a boy's relationship with his father and his gender identity—his sense of himself as masculine and his identification with men—cannot be ignored. The legacy of masculine confidence is either passed to or withheld from the son, and the results can be seen in the way he relates to men throughout life.

The studies referred to in Chapter 5 showed that a pattern of unsatisfactory father-son relationships often precedes homosexuality. I'm deliberately using the term "unsatisfactory relationship" rather than "bad father," "rejecting father," or similar terms. Too often we place blame on the *individual* rather than the *relationship*, somehow indicting the father as though he purposefully inflicted pain on his son. In fact, few fathers knowingly reject or hurt their children, and fewer still are guilty of deliberate cruelty. In this sense, the problems occurring between father and son may be no one's fault. A father may have been absent out of necessity, leaving the son feeling deliberately abandoned. Or a father may have been limited, incapable of showing the affection or attention the child needed. A boy may have been born with a sensitive nature, reading rejection or coldness into a father who was in fact accepting and available. Miscommunication, as well, is often the culprit. A father's actions or words can be misread, again creating a misperception in the child's mind. No matter, the end result is the same: A boy perceives the father to have a certain attitude toward him, and he responds emotionally to that perception. More often than not, no one is to bless or to blame.

If we must blame anything, it should be the chain of events beginning from infancy which shape a boy's attitude toward father, men, and himself. Those events begin with a son's earliest perceptions of his father, perceptions which the average adult probably can't remember but which had profound effects on his development. A favorable perception of a father's attitude will build confidence in a son. That confidence encourages him to relate freely to father, male siblings, mentors, or teachers and friends. It's as though an emotional baton is passed between the significant males in a boy's life. With each passage he grows more secure, because he gets consistent reassurance from each man he relates to. Without that passage he's crippled to a degree, has less reassurance, and experiences more insecurity.

Interrupting the Chain

Of course, this chain can be interrupted either favorably or unfavorably. A boy can feel unloved by his father, making him hesitant to relate to other men. But another important male might enter his life whose acceptance and interest could undo that hesitancy. That may set his course in a different direction, from insecurity to increased confidence in spite of early problems with his father. Likewise, even a strong foundation in a father's love can be undermined by serious rejection or hostility from other men, although the chance of enduring that sort of rejection is better for the boy who has already had a good start with his father. At any rate, the early interactions between father and son lay the groundwork for future male-to-male relations which influence a man's gender identity.

To you, men perhaps seemed distant, unavailable, rejecting. Fear or resentment of them may have been a part of your response to that perception, and that response created an increased need for male love. When that need became sexual, you satisfied it through homosexuality. Then, when you realized that homosexual relationships were in conflict with your desire to please God, you gave them up. But you didn't give up the longings for men you had felt for so long. In fact, they have hopefully become stronger than ever.

I say "hopefully" because those longings will motivate you to sustain the kind of relationships that will be a source of healing. Your perception of yourself as a man and of your relations to other men will change as you experience male love in its full, true form.

"Male love" may sound erotic to some; to others it might sound downright silly. But if you think about it, it's something all men need, and something most men seek. Not through romance or sentiment, but through strong bonding and committed friendship.

But male love isn't going to get your address and track you down. You have to put yourself into places and situations where it can be found and experienced. In short, you need to *integrate*.

Over 80 percent of my male clients have expressed dissatisfaction with their social life, especially with other men. Many of them had virtually no social relationships with men, while others had some contact with them but felt there was much to be desired in their same-sex friendships. In general, they have felt threatened by men, or have tended to idealize certain males to a high degree and cling to them exclusively at the expense of other friendships, or have felt real hostility toward men, getting close to them for a time but then cutting them off early in the friendship. In all cases, pursuing more satisfying relationships with their own sex improved their perception of themselves, induced a different response toward men, and decreased their sexual attractions to them.

Integration, then, is a vital part of growth. And it's no coincidence that better relationships with men accompany less sexual attraction toward them.[1]

Healthy Men

Having confronted your current relationships and corrected the parts of them needing correction, you move on toward new relationships, or new ways to relate, or both. That's what integration is all about. Integration happens when you develop on-going relationships with healthy men. I don't assume that you've never had a healthy relationship with a man, but I will assume that you haven't had *enough* intimacy with men. Your attraction to sexual encounters with them speaks of a need, one that remains and still looks for satisfaction.

Let's clarify this concept of "healthy men." "Health" is a very subjective term. To a degree, all of us are unhealthy. As long as we're imperfect, a fact I hope you won't dispute, we're unhealthy in some ways. So in that sense there are no perfectly healthy men. But there are men who are generally healthy, men who are secure in their gender identity, who experience normal sexual attractions to women, and who are confident and comfortable with other men. Additionally, they're reasonably stable, living moderate, exemplary lifestyles and making valid contributions to their communities. They are, in other words, men worth emulating and identifying with.

Are they better than you? Hardly. You may already have many of their qualities, even if you don't realize it. And there are probably qualities you have that are lacking in them. So you have much to contribute to them, just as they have a good deal to contribute to you. Integrating with them would be to your mutual benefit.

And yet, more often than not, Strugglers avoid healthy men. This is especially ironic because I believe each of them—including you—has the potential to be such a man. In fact, many Strugglers already are, in most ways, yet they don't know it. They don't identify with such men, feeling somehow unentitled to enjoy their company.

Often this happens because of the concepts that healthy men represent: male confidence, authority, strength. Those are the very qualities that a father represents to a growing boy. I'm convinced that, just as a Struggler will have felt alienated from his father early in life, he will likewise feel alienated from those qualities that his father represented *and* from other men who also represent them.

What kind of men have you felt most comfortable with? Your response will be revealing. I don't necessarily mean what kind of men you like and admire the most, but what kind you've felt *comfortable* with. Or, better yet, what kind of men do you feel entitled to socialize with and befriend?

I've found that boys experiencing gender-identity problems cling to other boys who seem nonthreatening or nonmasculine. They seem safe to each other, so they establish friendships based not on respect and admiration but on safety. As one of my counselees put it, "I normally hang out with geeks. The Normies scare me."

Normies represent the qualities you may admire and want for yourself, but you may also fear rejection or scorn from the men who have those qualities.

That's why integration with those guys is so vital! Until you experience normal relationships with them, which will include their acceptance of you and extension of friendship to you, you'll go on assuming you're not like them, or are less of a man than they are. And as long as that's your perception, you'll still respond with longings for love from men who represent all the qualities you felt were unavailable to you. Until you experience healthy male friendship, you'll go on longing for sexual love from idealized male figures. One way or another you're going to strive for masculine contact. Why not strive for it from the right source, in the right way?

The Continuing Need

I mentioned earlier the need a boy/man has for a Nurturer, a Mentor, and a Comrade, and pointed out the absence of these figures as playing a crucial role in the development of an insecure gender identity. I should point out, though, our *continuing* need for each of these figures. To a degree we always need them, and the need for each should not be taken as a sign of immaturity. Instead, it is the *degree of need* for each which determines our security and general health. So grown men, if they're honest, will admit a need to lean on another man for nurturing during particularly weak and stressful times. A certain amount of mentoring is also needed, as a man passes into different phases of his career and life experiences. And, of course, he will always need the security and challenge that comes with comradery.

But our development requires a certain emphasis on each of these. The male infant, for example, craves large doses of nurturing. Much of it will come from his mother, and rightfully so. But if the father is not nurturing the boy as well, he may develop a craving for male nurturing, along with a belief that it's not going to be available to him. That creates the perception, need, and response mentioned earlier: "I want a man's comfort and reassurance, but I can't have it, so there must be something wrong with me."

The young boy likewise needs mentoring, whether from a father or an older figure. Siblings, teachers, coaches, or older friends provide this vital part of development. And comrades are always needed, especially when a child has reached a level of security achieved through his relationship with a nurturing male and a mentor.

A man will crave the kind of relationship he's lacked, whether early in life or throughout life. That craving, far from being unnatural, is a good, healthy striving for the very thing the man needs. And that striving should be identified, respected, and satisfied. Your integration should include nurturing, mentoring, and comradery, with an emphasis on the kind of relationship you have the strongest desire for.

Male Nurturing

Male nurturing is a boy's earliest experience of his father's love. Infants are, ideally, accepted unreservedly by their dads. In a healthy family, a father gives his infant son unqualified affection and attention. He delights in his boy, cooing over him and regarding him with admiration. He displays open affection for the child, comforting him, playing with him, and—very important—actively pursuing him. He makes his son feel wanted and sought after, a prize and delight to his father.

If this nurturing was not expressed or perceived by the child, he will go on craving it. If he didn't get it from Dad, he'll look elsewhere. His body may grow, but he will retain the unsatisfied longings for nurturing from a strong father figure, even when he himself is old enough to be a father.

Some would call this childishness. I call it legitimate hunger. And legitimate hunger can be satisfied at any stage of life. If you crave male nurturing, I suggest that you find it rather than be ashamed of your need for it, because that need isn't going anywhere. It will remain a part of you as long as it remains unsatisfied. Satisfaction, in this case, comes by finding a male nurturer.

Nurturers aren't hard to find. They're pastors, therapists, ministry leaders—any kind of man who dedicates himself, professionally or privately, to the welfare of other men. He's easy to spot: He extends himself, whether by presenting himself specifically as someone who is available to help others or else by his interactions with other men. There is a strength about him tempered with warmth which draws others to him, and he is known, at least implicitly, as a father figure. He is someone you can look up to and lean on.

The key element of your relationship with him is *safety*. A Nurturer is there to provide a safe place to expose your conflicts, to be honest about your feelings without fear of retaliation or rebuke. He is perhaps the one person you can let your guard down with, the one who's available to listen to all your frustrations without making you feel stupid for having them. In fact, in his presence you feel highly valued no matter what you're going through. He expresses consistent goodwill to you, encouraging you without being patronizing, offering sympathy without degrading you. He believes in you.

Knowing that gives you a special kind of encouragement.

Obviously your bond with a Nurturer is like a recreation of the father-son relationship. Some might say it's like having the father you never had; I say just the opposite. Relating to a Nurturer means, sooner or later, experiencing some of the unfinished business between you and your natural father. That signals the therapeutic experience called "transference," one that is common between counselor and counselee but can also occur between a man and another man who becomes a significant father figure to him. "Transference" means the transferring of strong perceptions, responses, and unresolved conflicts between you and someone from the past onto someone in the present. It's a psychoanalytical term describing the patient's response to the analyst when the patient may view the analyst the way he viewed his father (or other important figures from his early years). He may assume that the analyst feels toward him the way his father did, and will respond accordingly. So a patient who always felt demeaned by his father will eventually feel that his analyst is also demeaning him. He will read contempt into the analyst's facial expressions, or interpret his remarks as being sarcastic or overly critical. I see this phenomenon happen in both professional and nonprofessional relationships.

Father Figures

When I was 16 I began attending Calvary Chapel of Costa Mesa, California. That was in 1971, when the "Jesus movement" was in full swing. There was an astounding revival happening in the hippie culture, with thousands of long-haired, blue-jeaned kids responding to the gospel and flooding the churches, Calvary Chapel in particular. Although the force behind the movement was definitely Jesus Christ, the man most commonly associated with it was Chuck Smith, Calvary's pastor. He offered genuine acceptance to the hippies along with a simple, no-nonsense approach to the Bible. But whether we realized it or not, we were attracted not only to Chuck's solid teaching but to the solid father figure he represented as well. Remember, this was a time of real (and unfortunate) alienation between kids and their parents. Many of Chuck's young parishioners had entered the hippie movement during a stage of rebellion, causing or caused by a strong rift with their families. Though Christianity changed their perspective of life and morality, many retained their sense of distance from their fathers and mothers. To them, Chuck was a surrogate—a patient and accepting father figure, easy to idealize and trust.

I've always been interested in the way men respond to Chuck. Back in '71 I could sense the kind of relationships my friends had with their fathers by the way they reacted to him. Some were literally terrified of him, for no good reason. Of course, we're all a bit intimidated by someone we greatly admire, and there's much to admire in Chuck. But this was something more. I saw kids freeze like scared rabbits when he would walk by, somehow afraid he "saw right through them," as one friend put it, and didn't approve of what he saw. Others just stared at him in wide-eyed awe, much as one would admire a knight or a warrior. Still others would put unfair and unrealistic expectations on him. They would demand some special attention from him (he ministered, and still ministers, to a few thousand people per service—how much attention does the man have to spare?) and if they didn't get it they would feel devastated. They took it as a personal rejection. They were, in fact, transferring onto Chuck the problems they had had with their own fathers. And when they recognized what they were doing, and took responsibility for it, they matured.

That's the value of a nurturing relationship. Not only does it give you a chance to experience acceptance and comfort from a caring man, but it also lets you re-experience early conflicts, identify them, and discuss them openly. I've come to see this as a turning point in my own clients' progress. Much of the early counseling phase is pleasant enough, because the counselee is learning about himself and enjoying the safety and empathy that our relationship offers. But sooner or later I disappoint my clients. It's inevitable. Either I err one way or another, or the client begins to perceive me as he used to perceive his own father. Suddenly I'm no longer the Good Counselor but Jack the Ripper, M.A. That used to terrify me; now I see it as an opportunity to work and grow with the client. And in so doing our relationship becomes stronger and more productive.

So if you need a Nurturer—a father figure, if you will—find one. But don't expect perfection. You wouldn't really mature if you had it, anyway, because we grow up emotionally when we accept the limitations of people we rely on without rejecting them.

The Mentor Role

There's a fine line between Nurturers and Mentors. Although a certain amount of teaching may come from a Nurturer, his primary role is to provide comfort, affection, and reassurance. Similarly, a Mentor might provide some nurturing, but his primary role is to provide teaching and encouragement toward certain goals. The emphasis on one or the other is what distinguishes a Nurturer from a Mentor.

In *The McGill Report on Male Intimacy,* Dr. Michael McGill refers to this distinction by saying:

> This strange combination of parent and peer seems to be the unique feature of these male mentor relationships. A mentor offers a man the guidance of a parent, the compassion of a peer without the competition.[2]

Mentors fill an important need in developing boys. They are still, of course, looking up to men or older boys in general. But they're also becoming independent enough to need less of their father's unconditional nurturing. They look for other men to emulate, men they can admire and identify with. Of course, they may admire and identify with their father, but they also need to spread out and test their abilities to relate to other admired male figures.

Other cultures are smarter than ours in this respect. Some tribal communities, for example, make a definite ritual out of same-sex identification and bonding. When their young men reach puberty, the other men take them out and initiate them, through various rites, into masculine society. Boys know they're accepted by older men, making the transition from boyhood to adolescence one of honor and security.

A Mentor, then, is a male who functions as a teacher and a guide. In childhood an older brother often serves as a mentor. Men outside the family, as well, fill the mentoring role. That's why there's a double value to boyhood experiences like music lessons, schooling, and athletics. They expose a boy to male figures who fine-tune his abilities while increasing his confidence with men in general. As a child is made secure through the acceptance and reassurance he gets from the Nurturer, he can move on to the mentoring relationship, which is a bit more demanding. There again the fine line is drawn between Mentorer and Nurturer: A Mentor is a male that a boy wants to emulate and learn from, not just bond with.

When you find someone with experience and proficiency in a part of life you'd like to improve in, and when that person is willing to help guide you into more expertise in that area, you've found a Mentor. That part of life may be a specific skill, or it may be a way of expressions. (Some men, for instance, look for Mentors to help them develop more masculine ways of expressing themselves.) Like nurturing, mentoring is a valuable experience which satisfies a legitimate need.

In the legend of the Knights of the Round Table, a young knave called Percible was fascinated by the knight Sir Lancelot. Lancelot represented so much of what Percible wanted to have—bravery, competence, honor. So Percible sought him out as a Mentor. He chased Lancelot, literally, until he convinced him to take him on as an apprentice. Through Lancelot, Percible learned the skills of knighthood and eventually was inducted into the company of the Round Table. Percible had the desire and potential to become a Knight; Lancelot's willingness to mentor him bridged the gap between his desire and his knighthood. This legendary form of mentoring is worked out in hundreds of ways in modern life.

Mentors in Real Life

Eight years ago I decided to try some serious weight-lifting. I had always admired the discipline of body-builders, not to mention the physiques they carried around like trophies. My admiration turned into a personal challenge, so I decided to quit simply admiring these guys and start trying to be like them. As usual, I plunged right into the thick of things without a lot of forethought or preparation, and joined what's known as a "hard-core gym" that was owned by a former Mr. America. I'd already tried health spas, which I decided were "too tame"; I wanted to really get into some intense, blood-and-guts bodybuilding.

Ever walk into a room full of gorillas in tank tops? I was astounded. In magazines, these guys look larger than life; in person, they *are* larger than life! When I joined up with them, I felt like I'd crashed a party of Greek gods; pencilnecks like me were definitely not invited. Still, I forced myself to change into my workout gear and get with the program. Never did it occur to me that I might ask for some help with the equipment, or get some tips from these accomplished athletes. I was too scared of them, too ashamed of my own inexperience to admit I had no idea what I was doing there.

So for four months I ducked into the gym six days a week, acknowledging no one, pretending I was entirely self-sufficient, and fooling nobody but myself. Naturally I made slow progress, and succeeded in doing little but exhausting myself with minimal results. The owner finally approached me in the middle of my workout and rather graciously remarked, "You know, if you keep training that way you're going to cause me some real insurance problems!" That was, as they said in *Casablanca,* the start of a beautiful friendship. A few quick lessons from him made all the difference, and afforded me some confidence and comfort when I went to the gym. My Mentor bridged the gap between me and the men I wanted to emulate, freeing me to at least try to be like them.

That's what Mentors are for. If there's an area of life you want to excel in, find someone who already excels in it and ask for help. The technical benefit of this will be your increased ability in a certain area. The long-term benefit will be an increased confidence in your masculinity and a deepened security in your gender identity. Remember, gender identity is your sense of yourself as being masculine, and masculinity is enhanced each time you conquer an old fear and adopt a new form of behavior.

The Comrade Role

A Comrade is a companion, the kind of friend usually described as a "buddy" with whom you have an ongoing, intimate bond. It is a relationship based on commonality— common goals, common ideals and principles, and a common interest in investing time and energy into a friendship. The ability to make and maintain such a friendship comes again from a certain amount of confidence. As a boy becomes less dependence on his father's nurturing and gains more confidence by learning from his Mentor, he can establish relationships with equals, or peers. With his peers he learns to compete, to be challenged, to find common ground and to bond. This bonding with peers will have begun in childhood, hopefully, but in adolescence it becomes especially important.

The adolescent has become less emotionally dependent on his parents and places more importance on his peer relationships. That's probably why adolescence is a time of such struggle between parents and teenagers: The parents lose some (or a lot) of their clout, and the approval of peers means more to the teenagers than his parents' approval does. Conformity marks adolescence. Dressing, talking, and acting like "the other guys" becomes vital to the teenager, and often the bizarre ways that teenagers express themselves are just statements of independence from their parents. Peer relations, or relations with Comrades, are as vital to a healthy gender identity as nurturing and mentoring.

But if nurturing and mentoring haven't occurred, the adolescent boy is ill-equipped to deal with the challenge of peer relationships. That can turn the teenage years into a nightmare of self-doubt and rejection. In fact, many men I've worked with point to their adolescence as a high point of misery in their lives. Lacking the assurance of a solid father-son relationship, they shy away from other boys as well. And other boys certainly don't encourage them to do any differently. Kids are, all too often, cruel. They sniff out insecurity in a boy and crucify him for it, only encouraging him to avoid efforts at integration with his own kind. That solidifies the boy's long-held perception that he is indeed an outcast, unacceptable to other boys and men in general.

That, combined with our culture's lack of emphasis on male relationships, creates real problems for the Struggler. All men need other men. We need male friendships that are solid and lasting, yet over and over again we ignore this need or even deny its existence! Strange but true, the American male is often a friendless creature who could learn a lot from his female counterpart. In this area women have us beat, because they seem more aware of their need for each other and are more willing to express it. "In our society," says Elliot Engel, "it seems as if you've got to have a bosom to be a buddy." How sad for all of us.

How sad for you especially, though. If most men have an unsatisfied need for comradery, your need for it is doubly strong. If homosexuality is a sexualized emotional need for intimacy, then its resolution can only come when you are getting, without sex, the male intimacy you've been looking for. The answer is not to stop looking, but to look harder.

Finding a Comrade

Looking means using a little common sense and an understanding of the way men bond in our culture. Man-to-man relationships usually depend on an indirect activity—sports, for example—to keep them going. Seldom do men admit to each other the need they have for each other, covering it up with phrases like "Let's play golf" instead of "Let's get together—we need to build our friendship." (Did you notice how funny that sounded? Even I winced a little as I wrote it; that says a lot about our attitude toward male bonding.)

Of course, if this is a problem for men in general it's especially a problem for *you.* Since men, even healthy ones, aren't prone to extend open invitations to bonding, it makes it that much more difficult for you to determine how to get close to the men you need. You can't just walk up to a fellow and say, "Hey, you represent all the qualities of masculinity I've had a sexualized need to merge with. Wanna bond?"

You can't just request time and friendship from other men. But you can, indirectly at first, become a part of their lives by joining them when they're together. That is the safest and most effective way I know to begin integrating—through male group activities.

The problem with this is that male group activities often bring to mind some of the most unnerving moments of childhood and adolescence. Those were times boys bonded through sports, for example, something many Strugglers were terrified of. (I've got my own ideas about this. I can't believe that homosexual desires impair anyone's athletic abilities; in fact, gay men in discos can dance like gymnasts for hours on end! But since a boy with gender-related problems may feel uncomfortable with other boys, it's his discomfort, not lack of ability, that stifles his physical performance.) So to integrate with men in groups, you've got to get past your fear of group activities. More specifically, you have to overcome the fear that you'll again be humiliated when you try to "play with the guys."

Of course, "playing with the guys" needn't mean sports activities. It can include any kind of group activity that men are participating in. Your job is to find one that's compatible with you. Comrades are found among men, and your relationship with one is built when you've given yourself a chance to meet men, make acquaintances, let the acquaintances evolve into friendships, and let the friends become comrades.

You do this by putting yourself in situations where this can happen. (A hard first step, but a necessary one.) Then you look for men within the group who seem friendly and receptive to you. That's not too hard; just keep your eyes open and, as Solomon said, show yourself to be friendly. When the door to conversation seems open, pursue it. If you're shy, as many Strugglers are, you may experience a thousand anxieties at this point. But keep in mind the fact that nobody can see those anxieties but you, so don't let them stop you. As you gradually gain acceptance and sense a desire on another man's part to know you better, follow through.

You might feel awfully strange doing this. It can be reminiscent of "cruising," putting the "make" on another man in a sexual sense. Yet there is such a thing as healthy, nonsexual pursuit. Don't back off from it. It's the very thing you need.

The Challenge of Integration

Integration is a challenge, one you'll have to accept if you're going to make progress. Only through relationships do we grow; without them we stagnate. Begin by deciding what kind of man-to-man relationship you're needing the most—nurturing, mentoring, comradery, or all three. Then make a commitment to aggressively pursue what you need, and the kind of man you need it from.

Yes, pursue. I can almost hear someone snickering. "This sounds like some sort of husband-hunting manual!" Not quite, because it's nonsexual, nonromantic love you're looking for. But if you aren't willing to actively look for it, there's no reason to assume you'll ever have it. And if you never have it, you'll never get past the need for it. So go for it; you don't really have a choice.

You may balk at this idea. You may retain a childish wish that someone will come along and, seeing how much you need male bonding, offer himself like some kind of nurturing White Knight and say, "Hey, little boy, I'll give you a hand." Don't count on it. No one can see your needs, and most people will never assume you have them. It's up to *you* to create an environment for yourself that will allow relationships to build and grow.

If all of this sounds like nothing more than a "how to make friends and influence people" speech, remember the ultimate goal of integration: to change the early perceptions of yourself that created sexual responses to men in the first place. I'm convinced that those perceptions will only change by getting a new, healthy response from other people, and that this response will only come when you integrate with them.

That's how it all started. You perceived a response, and your perception shaped your gender identity. To change your perception, you need accepting, positive responses from the kind of men you value and admire. As they favorably respond to you, you begin to see yourself differently. Your confidence grows, your identification with healthy men becomes more solid, and your need for male love begins to be satisfied. And that's when healing occurs—when the needs you've tried to meet indirectly through sex are being met directly through nonsexual intimacy.

10

Overfocus

When the changes you want are slow in coming, and you're doing all you can to effect change, the first thing to look at is your perspective. One of my major goals in writing this book was to address not only homosexuality, but the larger issues of life that have contributed to it or arise from it. Which begs the question: Is a change in your sexual orientation the most important thing in life?[1]

If it is, you may be suffering from what I call *overfocus*. Overfocus occurs when a particular issue becomes an obsession, much like a toy to a child ("I'll just die if I can't have that!"). The obsession becomes the filter through which one sees all of life. And just as indulgence in anything can become an obsession, so can change ("I'll just die if I don't get over this!").

Of course, as Christians we are mandated to make no compromise with sin or weakness. But our broader and foremost goal must always be to know, love, and become like Christ. Overfocus prevents this because it takes its victim's eyes off Christ and puts them onto "The Big Problem Which Is Still There!" And when the Big Problem looms over all other issues, it remains unsolved. Overfocus is a paradox: So much time and energy is invested in worrying about a problem that the problem is kept alive!

Overfocus is characterized by an inability to see yourself outside of your "issue." Your issue and your identity become one and the same. When you see yourself as "a person struggling against homosexuality" rather than "a person" or, more specifically, a child of God, then your identity is faulty. You're defining yourself by one area and neglecting to see your entire personality and potential.

Part of the blame for overfocus lies with our penchant for labels and with the trend of pop-psychology to create new problems, convince us that we have them, and exhort us to "recover" from them. These days you're nobody if you're not an Adult Child of Somebody, or a Recovering Whatever, or a Survivor of Something Quite Awful. Personal issues are the status symbols of the oh-so-sensitive enlightened elite, without which one can hardly be introduced.

My sarcasm is not meant to trivialize the legitimate and deep pain of, for example, Adult Children of Alcoholics or Survivors of Incest. Such groups are legitimate and serve people with tremendous needs. But our penchant for labelling actually demeans the seriousness of these groups, and sometimes borders on the ridiculous. (I, for one, am incensed to hear about a new *Christian* book subtitled "Understanding and Hope for Adult Children of Evangelicals."[2] Is my evangelicalism really taken to be a blight on my children's future?)

In such a climate it's no surprise that the Fighter falls prey to overfocus. Yet as long as homosexuality is the focal point of your identity, you'll exhibit the next characteristic of overfocus, which is heightened anxiety over one issue combined with apathy about other, more important matters. Getting over occasional homosexual fantasies, for example, seems deathly urgent, but making friends and planning for the future seem relatively unimportant. But worrying about homosexuality, or craving freedom from it, doesn't do anything to reduce it. In fact, it increases its influence over your thoughts and behavior. Worse still, overfocus prevents you from making the changes in other areas of life which will eventually bring about changes in your sexual orientation. So a vicious cycle indeed is begun: You worry obsessively about existing homosexual attractions and do little or nothing to address the factors that contribute to your homosexuality! It's a bit like the person who moans day and night about being overweight, so preoccupied with his body fat that he takes no time to exercise and plan his diet, the two key methods for reducing fat.

Defining yourself by unwanted sexual feelings also increases self-loathing as opposed to genuine humility. Humility is important to a Christian—God resists the proud and shows grace to the humble (Psalm 138:6). But humility is not a self-loathing state ("I'm just a disgusting pervert!") but a realization of our human weakness in contract to God's greatness. Truly humble people are not obsessed with themselves in a positive or a negative way; they realize their imperfections and rely on the grace of God to enable them to change what they can, as much as they can.

The presence of these characteristics is a good sign of narrow, overfocused perspective. Remember, homosexuality is not resolved as long as it is an object of obsession.

Remember, too, that the presence of homosexual desires is not an indication that change hasn't occurred. It is not just the disappearance of homosexuality that we've been aiming for, but a reduction in the intensity and frequency of same-sex attractions, and in the control they have over your thoughts and behavior. Some Fighters will always have, to some degree, sexual thoughts and feelings that they would rather not have. The same can be said of all of us. None of us will ever be exempt from temptation of some sort, and it is unrealistic and unbiblical to assume otherwise.

My experience has been that most Fighters who are consistent and motivated do experience lasting, significant changes, both in their sexual attractions and their lives in general. But when change tarries or does not occur as we wish it would, some pitfalls should be avoided.

Self-pity is the most common. I've written extensively about the unfairness of the Fighter's predicament, and I in no way negate my prior remarks by stating that nobody starts or finishes life getting everything he wants. We all lack something we wish we had; we all have something we'd rather do without. To a degree, we're all unsatisfied with our lot but, in the long run, our success in life will be determined by our perspective and our refusal to give in to self-pity when life seems unfair.

Van Den Aardweg emphasizes the role self-pity plays in the Fighter's life. His form of therapy, in fact, is called "Anti-Complaining Therapy," in which he encourages his patients to learn to laugh at their complaints and their defeatist, pitiful attitudes (Van Den Aardweg, 1986). He feels that homosexuality has its roots in infantile self-pity, a self-pity which must be abandoned if sexual health is to be achieved.

While I cannot say that I believe self-pity is always the root issue, I certainly see a tendency toward it in many. Just as children on a car trip are prone to keep repeating, "When are we gonna get there?" so Fighters may be prone to whine, "When am I gonna get better?"

Again, the paradox: The more we whine about changes that are not occurring, the more we feed the immaturity expressed through such whining. Blocked maturity means that nothing, sexuality included, will get better.

Paul had a similar problem, detailed in 2 Corinthians 12:7-10. He described it as a "thorn in the flesh," something that buffeted him and caused him considerable discomfort. We cannot say what the "thorn" was, though we've certainly been guessing at it over the centuries! But precisely what his problem was isn't the point of the narrative. Paul was reminding us that, at some point, we may all suffer a continued problem or condition which we know is unhealthy, and which we've earnestly worked on and prayed about, but which persists nonetheless.

After Paul prayed three times about his "thorn," God spoke to him, saying "My grace is sufficient for you, for My strength is made perfect in weakness."

What was God saying? That Paul was doomed to forever suffer with this thing? Not necessarily. We don't know whether he continued to carry this problem or was eventually relieved of it. All we know is that, for a time, God deliberately allowed the "thorn" to continue to buffet Paul and that he was actually a better man for it.

No, I don't think homosexuality is necessarily a "thorn in the flesh." But the principle still applies. Whatever our weakness is, we cannot demand that we be relieved of it. Nor can we give in to it. We can only accept its presence, for the time being, and live our lives as fully as we can in spite of it.

Ultimate Issues

There comes a point when all of us decide which is more important: happiness or destiny. The quest for happiness takes into account our feelings and wants, and requires that both be satisfied. Destiny emphasizes stewardship: What is my calling in life? What am I here to accomplish before I die, and how can I accomplish it? It may sound cold, even inhumane, to say destiny is more important than happiness. But in fact it's more inhumane to commend personal happiness as a goal because it will never be fully attained.

The search for happiness is essentially a search for a feeling—a sense of well-being, pleasure, satisfaction. The feeling is largely produced and maintained by circumstances and events. When things go as you wish, you're happy. When they don't, you lose the feeling. To maintain happiness means to make sure things go as you want them to, which requires more control over events than any of us have, so naturally happiness fluctuates and frustration sets in.

The search for happiness also begets the search for perfection, which is never attained in this life. So the Fighter who insists he or she cannot be happy until all homosexual tendencies are gone, is saying, in essence, "I demand perfection in this part of my life." But the demand never stops there. Perfectionism in one area must spill over into others, and that's when the tyranny of perfectionism takes over. Some area of life will always be imperfect. If perfection is necessary for fulfillment, fulfillment cannot be attained. And so the man seeking fulfillment remains sadly unfulfilled.

Destiny is another matter. The search for personal destiny begins when a person says, as Paul did at his conversion, "Lord, what would you have me to do?" And when the knowledge of our calling in life, and our efforts to fulfill that call, become primary to us, we experience the fulfillment we cannot attain as long as we seek it.

It is of relatively minor importance whether or not I'm "happy." Far more important is my effectiveness as a husband, father, friend, and counselor. And of course, when I'm diligent to fulfill my calling in these areas, I'm a very happy man indeed. And when my faults are made known to me, my responsibility is to do all I can to improve, knowing that my best efforts will not produce perfect results.

The eternal perspective—that's what gets people through their struggles, not the insistence that the struggles themselves end. And that brings us to perhaps the most important point: All of us will stand before God to give Him an account of what we did with ourselves. That is a part of our destiny we cannot avoid:

> For we must all appear before the judgment seat of Christ, that each one may receive the things done in the body, according to that he has done, whether good or bad (2 Corinthians 5:10).

The things done in your body—that's stewardship. You will not be held responsible for the material you were given to begin your life with. Your emotions may have been damaged, your early experiences devastating and crippling. You may have developed personal wounds you carry to this day. And yes, your sexual desires may at times be in conflict with the norm.

But you will not be judged for any of these things. You'll be rewarded, eternally, for what you did with what you were given. Not how completely you were healed, but how faithful you were.

Imagine yourself in God's presence, standing in the company of thousands of other saints, ready to answer for your life. Knowing you were a Fighter, He asks:

> "Did you repent of sexual sin and was your repentance real?"

> "Did you resist temptation when it came?"

> "Did you take what steps you could to improve the gift of sexuality I gave you?"

"Did you faithfully conform your behavior to My will, even when your desires told you to do otherwise?"

These are the ultimate issues you're grappling with, the ones which determine whether or not you're winning both the battle and the war. Avoid the tendency to overfocus, because it will always distort your perspective and your perception. If you insist on complete freedom from all unwanted desires, and you insist on it ASAP, you're dooming yourself to frustration and defeat. But if you will strive to someday answer "yes" to the above questions, then you can consider yourself a Fighter who's coming out ahead.

11

Childhood Trauma and Female Sexuality

by Dr. Carol Ahrens, Ph.D.

Much of what you've read so far applies to both sexes. The principles of repentance, integrity, and the change process certainly work for women as well as men. But there are some issues that are specific to women, and this book would not be complete without giving them some attention. For that reason I am pleased to have been asked to contribute my thoughts in this chapter.

Having worked extensively with many women, I have found that certain problems are more common among women than men. In spite of the growing movement to abolish alleged differences between the sexes, we must admit that differences do exist. Not just physical differences, mind you, but specific contrasts in emotional responses and needs. Those contrasts become quite clear when we examine women dealing with lesbianism and compare them to men who struggle against homosexuality. Both groups deal with problems; some of those problems are common to both men and women, while some of them are more common among one sex than the other.

For example, promiscuity is found more frequently among homosexual men than among lesbians. That doesn't mean there is no such thing as a promiscuous lesbian; rather, it indicates that some behaviors are more likely to show up in one or the other sex. Likewise, lesbian relationships seem to be founded on emotional rather than physical attraction, whereas male homosexual relationships often begin with mutual physical admiration.

With these distinctions in mind, I would like to pay particular attention to a problem I commonly see among my female counselees who are in conflict over their sexuality: childhood abuse and its long-term effects.

Childhood Abuse: Its Nature and Its Effects

The effects of abuse are of special interest to me, both as a therapist and as a woman. As a therapist, I know that our identities are formed in infancy and early childhood, when we are in a position of total vulnerability. Traumas occurring during this crucial period have incredible, lasting effects on our relationships. And as a woman, I know there are special needs that little girls have that make them unique. When those needs are denied, ignored, or exploited, the future womanhood of that child is in jeopardy.

Just how are those needs denied, ignored, or exploited? Through abuse. I know you may be thinking, "Wait a minute. Abuse means some ghastly form of physical torture, doesn't it? That's a far cry from denying or ignoring a child's needs!" Not necessarily. Abuse can be overt, as in physical or sexual abuse, or it may be more subtle. Of course, its more subtle versions wouldn't legally qualify as child abuse, but they are forms of abuse nonetheless, and they have far-reaching consequences. One of those consequences is a distorted sexual identity. I have seen, time and again, clear connections between early abuse and confusion in sexuality. And I cannot ignore the histories of the many women I've known who have survived one form of abuse or another and are also attracted to other women. Although abuse by itself does not cause lesbianism, it can certainly be found in the background of many lesbian women and has in many cases been a contributing factor to their orientation. So let's look at the various forms abuse can take, the way those forms may affect your feminine identity, and ways you can overcome the effects of abuse.

I've seen abuse occur most often in one of three forms: physical abuse, sexual abuse, and emotional abuse. Each of these forms creates a profound wounding to the child which she carries into adulthood and which affects her ability to relate to both men and women.

Physical Abuse

Physical abuse—or, more specifically, physical child abuse—is such a shocking term that sometimes adults who were battered as children can't bring themselves to apply it to their childhood. That's because children who are physically abused can barely come to grips with the awful thing that is happening to them. They are suffering horribly at the hands of the very people who should be protecting them, but often they manage to protect their persecutors out of a sense of loyalty or guilt. They figure that Mom or Dad must always be right, no matter how strange their behavior seems, so they blame themselves. The result is a double tragedy. The child not only suffers physical damage, but she really believes there is something fundamentally wrong with her, and that she deserves to be mistreated.

Were you physically abused? If you're even asking yourself that question, it's entirely possible that you were. (Children who weren't abused would have no reason to ask it, after all.) According to the Child Welfare Services, 2.4 million cases of child abuse were reported in 1990. Besides being a terrifying statistic, that 2.4 million figure includes many children who don't even realize the harm that's been done to them. Perhaps they, like you, might grow into adulthood believing that nothing unusual happened to them. Incredibly, some children even believe that all other kids receive similar treatment from their parents. We all tend to think our childhood was normal, until we get the opportunity to honestly discuss our backgrounds and get input from others. Then we may realize that what we thought was normal was really abnormal, even destructive.

Comments I hear from my counselees are at times truly heartbreaking. "Was I abused?" they say. "Oh, no, not me. I was disciplined, of course. How? Oh, you know, with a razor strap or with switches. Sure, it hurt, and it would usually leave welts. And sometimes Dad had to lock me in a closet when I misbehaved, but it wasn't really abuse. I had it coming, I'm sure."

Ask yourself something: If you heard another person describe the way she was punished as a child, and if her treatment was similar to yours, how would you react? Would you be shocked, enraged, wanting to hug her and say, "Oh, how awful"? That tells you something about yourself. Perhaps you excuse the abuse you received, but would condemn it if it happened to someone else. That's a good indication that you too are a victim.

Does abuse automatically lead to lesbianism? Of course not. Many women who were battered as children have no sexual attractions to other women. But they develop other problems later in life. Homosexuality is like so many other things—it can be a result of certain factors that might, in some people, lead to same-sex attractions. In other people they may lead to other things. My point is that, if you are homosexual and have been abused, there may very well be a connection between the two. If the abuse came from a woman (mother, stepmother, etc.) you may be longing for the womanly love you so badly needed. If it came from a male you may have decided, consciously or not, that men are tyrants and should be avoided. These problems can and often do contribute to lesbian desires.

Knowledge like this may be threatening to you. It may shake your entire way of viewing yourself and your family. And who wants that? Yet the truth is, if you're a victim of physical abuse, you probably have ideas about yourself that are false, and that play into your ability to relate to people in a healthy way. Until you face this, these false ideas will overshadow your attempts to move into a healthy, secure identity as a woman.

By the way, I want it clear that I believe in discipline. I don't consider spanking in and of itself to be abusive. And I certainly don't want you to assume you've been abused if indeed you haven't. But I also know that, all too often, women dealing with lesbianism suffer from serious childhood trauma. As this book points out time and again, the trauma or pain behind homosexuality needs to be dealt with successfully before the homosexuality itself can be resolved. So if physical abuse is a part of your background, let me offer a few suggestions.

First, please consider therapy from a sound Christian counselor. I stress "Christian" because so many secular therapists leave the concepts of forgiveness and reconciliation out of their practice. You're a Christian, so your goal is not just to "get over" the effects of childhood abuse. It is also to forgive, to be reconciled if possible, and to continue to grow in grace and the knowledge of Christ. A Christian therapist can help you do just that, exploring the pain of your past from a biblical perspective. This is something that's difficult, if not impossible, to do with just anybody. Of course your friends are supportive of you, and you also have (I hope) a good pastor to turn to. But abuse is a special problem that really does require specialized treatment. So give some thought to counseling.

Second, expect to go through a period of deep anger, even rage. When you realize the wrong that was done to you, and its far reaching effects, you may become furious. Believe it or not, that's not only understandable but it can be to your benefit. Anger can be a great motivator, a force that makes us take action to ensure that we will no longer be victims, but conquerors. Many women, for example, become so angry when they face their abusive backgrounds that they determine to never allow themselves to be taken advantage of again. They choose their friends and prospective mates very carefully, and may even become involved in volunteer work with abused children. They use their anger to propel them into constructive, redemptive actions. So don't condemn yourself for being angry.

Finally, let yourself heal in God's good time. "When will the pain ever leave?" many women ask. "I blocked it out for so many years, but now that I've faced it I feel overwhelmed! Why doesn't it stop?" It will, I can assure you. But I can't say when. Nobody can. But I can say this: Your pain will, if you allow it to, create special sensitivity and strength in you. As you learn to cope with it, you learn so much about yourself as well! Isn't that one of the qualities of our Great High Priest Himself? He too has suffered, and so He comforts us in having had firsthand experience in pain. His suffering was awful, unspeakable, yet necessary for a higher purpose. Yours too can be turned into a tool for good. Begin praying now for God to show you how your sorrow can in time benefit others.

Sexual Abuse

Sexual abuse, like physical abuse, takes many different forms. Some girls are horribly raped, or forced to commit sexual acts against their will. Others are fondled, or coerced into exposing themselves. Sometimes they are victims of exhibitionism, during which others expose themselves or engage in inappropriate sexual behavior in the child's presence. Still others are seduced into activity that appears to be playful at first but then becomes erotic. These are all manifestations of sexual abuse, and all of them are deadly serious.

Worst of all, these crimes against children are often committed by family members or friends. The very people the girl has learned to trust become the ones who do lifelong damage to her, leaving her confused and violated.

When this violation occurs, several things happen to the girl, physically and emotionally. Physically, her God-given boundaries have been violated. Her body, which was intended to be kept under her own control, has been used for someone else's pleasure at her expense. This teaches her that she has no control, no power, not even over her own body. Her confidence in herself as a human being deserving respect and gentleness has been challenged, causing her to wonder what rights, if any, she really has. This confusion carries over into all her relationships, causing years of hardship.

Sexual abuse, like physical abuse, is often covered up, its existence denied by both perpetrator and victim. Some comments I hear in therapy bear this out:

> I don't know if this is important or not, but he [adult relative] used to take baths with me and sometimes sleep in my bed. He would touch me in certain places and I'm not sure what he was trying to do. Was I molested?

It wasn't abuse, because I sort of liked it. I
mean, it felt good, and I didn't tell him to stop.
At first I was scared, but I really started enjoying it. I can't blame him, because I liked it at
the time. (The client was ten, her abuser was
in his forties.)

Denial. It is perhaps the major obstacle to truth and
healing. Denial is that emotional mechanism that protects us from hard realities, realities that must be faced
before any progress can be made. Denial means safety,
because as long as you deny something exists, you don't
have to deal with it. But it also means restriction,
because as long as you deny something exists, it can
continue to damage you and keep you from growing.

Why do victims of sexual abuse so often deny its
impact? Why do they so often tell themselves and others
that the crime wasn't really a crime at all? Simple—
they are taught to deny. And you, if you are one of these
victims, have probably been taught to do the same. Most
likely the person who violated you didn't encourage you
to discuss it with anyone. In fact, he probably conveyed
the message to you that you should keep this a secret.
Sometimes that's done in a friendly way ("This is just
between us, O.K.?") or through a threat ("If you ever tell,
you'll be sorry."). You were confused, frightened, ashamed.
Maybe you blamed yourself. Or maybe you thought it
was normal. Or maybe (and this is common) you were
afraid to tell anyone because you didn't want to rock the
boat. You might have felt that your family would be hurt
if you let them know about it, so you kept it to yourself.
There's even a chance that you tried to tell, but you
weren't believed. Or you were ignored. Or it seemed as
though no one cared.

No matter how you may have been taught to deny the
trauma of sexual abuse, the fact is that your continued
denial of it will only make things worse. So admit it

now: If you were involved in any kind of sexual or erotic activity with an adult or with another child who was significantly older than you, then you are a victim of sexual abuse. As with physical abuse, sexual abuse can and often does play a key role in the development of lesbianism.

Since the offending parties in these situations are usually male, the girl who is sexually abused often develops certain ideas about men in general. They may be seen as exploitive, brutish, even dangerous. The association of the male body with a childhood trauma may make the thought of sex with men repulsive or frightening. Some women have come to me saying, "The men I've known are such jerks! They just used me. They're all alike, because they're only after one thing. You just can't trust them." How sad, and how inaccurate it is to put all men in the same category because of a terrible experience you may have had with one of them. And yet, considering the pain that sexual abuse causes, who can really blame a victim for feeling that way?

Women, on the other hand, are often seen by victims as safe, loving, and nonthreatening. And so, in many cases, a woman will turn to other women for the most intimate forms of comfort and bonding. In these cases the male sex represents pain and fear, so it's no surprise that the female sex appears more attractive and inviting.

What can you do about it? Several things. Start by putting away shame. So many women feel ashamed and guilty over events they had no control over. Even rape victims often feel such humiliation that they actually consider themselves to be dirty or, as some say, "damaged goods." You are in no way responsible for this tragedy. You were a child, innocent and trusting, who was horribly taken advantage of in the worst way. No matter what role you think you played in it, the fact remains that, even if you were a willing participant in sexual abuse, you were not capable of making an intelligent decision about your sexual expressions. The adult who violated you must take that responsibility, for the blame lies with him and him alone. Stop punishing yourself. Stop feeling guilty for the actions of others. And stop assuming that there is anything fundamentally wrong with you that may have brought this on.

Then get help. Professional help, if possible. But definitely talk about it to someone you can trust. Secrets like this are terrible burdens to bear, and there's no reason for you to go on bearing it alone. There may be Christian support groups in your area for victims of sexual abuse. Look into them, because there you may find an opportunity to open up to other women who have suffered the same injuries you have. You'll see that you are not alone, and you'll learn how others have coped with their past hurts.

Realize, too, that your sexuality is a precious gift that still exists. It may have been exploited, but that doesn't mean it's been destroyed. Like all facets of the human personality, it can be redeemed. If the thought of sexual expression with a man is threatening to you, don't push it. Don't rush out and date just to undo the wrong that's been done. Instead, slowly allow yourself to be built up again. Concentrate on friendships with both sexes, and give yourself all the time you need to learn to trust again. Eventually, as you regain the confidence that was taken from you early in life, you may feel the desire to become intimate with a husband. But that should never be your primary goal. Instead, your goal should be to grow, to heal, and to enjoy the benefits of loving, respectful relationships.

Emotional Abuse

Physical and sexual forms of abuse are marked by specific incidents, and are therefore easier to detect than emotional abuse. Emotional abuse is quite subtle, rather vague, and easily misinterpreted. Yet it exists, and it too has far-reaching consequences and effects on female sexual identity.

I want to be careful here, because you and I both know that all of us, in some way, have been emotionally abused to some degree. Everytime someone has said an unkind word to us, ignored us or embarrassed us in some way, we have technically been abused. Yet we wouldn't (I hope) go find a therapist or a support group for Victims of Rude Behavior. So let's not get carried away with these concepts.

But let's not ignore them either. Significant emotional abuse does happen, and when it happens to a child, she is wounded and does suffer.

Since emotional abuse—that is, behavior that creates significant emotional distress in another—occurs in too many forms to cover in one book, I'm going to focus on the forms of emotional abuse I've seen in the backgrounds of my clients. You will most likely be able to relate to one or more of them.

Rejection of a child's gender is something I've seen too many times. Parents of female infants often had hoped for a boy rather than a girl. In fact, I've known of mothers who wanted a boy so badly that, when their daughters were born, they refused to even hold them! Early bonding with our mothers is crucial to our development. It's our first experience of love and caregiving, so when we do without it, we're left with a huge emotional "hole in the soul."

In the film *Anne of the Thousand Days*, King Henry VIII was desperate for a son, having divorced his first wife because she couldn't give him one. His hopes lay with Anne Boleyn, a woman he had married in hopes of producing an heir to the throne. In an unforgettable scene, Anne is delivered of her first child with King

Henry, a baby girl. She looks up expectantly at her husband and says, "I've borne you a daughter, my Lord."

King Henry scowls, turning to leave the room without so much as looking at his daughter. Crushed, Anne protests, "But have you no kiss for your newborn child?"

"When my newborn child is a king, then will I kiss him," he replies as he stalks out.

Unbelievable? Not at all. It's more common than any of us would like to think. When I consider it, I feel sad and angry at the thought of a precious little girl being sent by God into the world, only to be devalued and ignored because of her sex. Some parents of these girls cut their hair into "boy" haircuts, gave them little boys' toys to play with, and dressed them like boys. In a way, their identity has been scorned by parents who were blinded to the beauty of a female child. No wonder these girls are confused about their sexuality!

This rejection profoundly affects the child. She gets the message that something about her is wrong. She considers herself to be the problem—more specifically, she considers her *sex* to be the problem. When it dawns on her that she "should" have been a boy, and that her femaleness has been rejected, she too learns to reject it. She absorbs her parents' wish for a boy and makes it her own, determining to be as "male" as she can. In such a case, she is simply set up to reject herself and to identify with men.

Another way emotional abuse appears is through abandonment. Between parent and child, abandonment happens when a parent is simply unavailable to the child. There may be very good reasons for the parent's unavailability. He or she may be overwhelmed with work responsibilities, or with problems that need attention, creating less time for the child. The problem is, the child doesn't realize that. All she knows is that Mom or Dad simply isn't there. Often she assumes it's because she herself is unloved and therefore unlovable.

When the abandonment, real or perceived, comes from the mother, the female child may develop a huge need for maternal care, combined with a determination to earn it. "If only I were a better girl," she may think, "or if only I tried harder, then I'd get the attention I want." And so she tries every trick in the book to get Mom's attention. Sadly, it doesn't work. Besides frustrating her desire to be a "good girl," this also intensifies her need for female love. She'll keep looking for it, perhaps finding it someday in the arms of another woman.

Then there's the emotional abuse of what I call "extension-making." Extension-making comes about when a mother uses her daughter to satisfy her own needs, rather than assuming responsibility for the satisfaction of her child's needs. On the surface this may look like simple overindulgence; on closer inspection, it shows itself to be something far more serious.

A mother may be unfulfilled in her marriage. Perhaps her husband works too hard, pays too little attention to her, or is simply distant emotionally. The wife is left in pain, feeling unloved and insignificant. She may then turn to her daughter, the one source of love that is readily available (and easily manipulated). Slowly, and perhaps without meaning to, she teaches her daughter to reverse roles and take care of her needs. She leans on her little girl, praising her when she fulfills her need, and rejecting her when she doesn't. The girl learns quickly that she'll be loved and rewarded with affection as long as she pleases Mom, so she jumps through all the right hoops, doing whatever it takes to be a "good girl." But being a good girl, in this case, means losing herself, having no idea who she is because she's so busy taking care of somebody else. She has become an extension of her mother, designed and used for the satisfaction of another person's personal, adult needs.

Her emotional survival is sustained by reading her mother, ascertaining what it is that Mom wants and how best to deliver it. In a real sense she is taking her father's place in the home by becoming her mother's prime source of emotional support and satisfaction. She becomes Mom's confidante, her caretaker, her comforter, her best friend. An adult might easily fulfill such a role, but it is far too much for a child to be expected to carry out. It can be, in a word, exhausting.

Of course, it can also seem nice and fulfilling for the child at times. She may feel very special, and very important because she is the center of Mom's affections and needs. But that role also exacts a terrible price—the forfeiting of personal identity development. The girl cannot bother with her own development; she's too busy second-guessing what her mother needs and becoming whatever Mom wants her to become. The "let me make you happy" routine becomes a lifestyle to her, a way of reassuring herself that she is important and loved.

In the midst of this "extension-making" the girl might well ask herself, "Why doesn't Daddy make Mom happy? Doesn't he know how? Boy, he's dumb/irresponsible/incapable of satisfying a woman's needs." In time that conviction may well develop into something broader: "Boy, men sure are dumb/irresponsible/incapable of satisfying a woman's needs." Do you think such a child is going to be anxious to bond with men? She has found in the home a way of feeling significant and loved (by pleasing Mom) and at the same time has seen first-hand how inept men can be.

If these situations sound familiar to you, I'd suggest that you have learned some false concepts about people and yourself. You've responded emotionally to these concepts by relating to men and women in certain ways, and your reaction to these concepts can be seen in the way you relate to others.

Unlearning the Lessons

All of these lessons are the legacy of a wounded childhood. And all of them can be unlearned through a process which will take you far toward resolving your conflicting desires.

First you grieve. There's nothing wrong with grief. We all grieve the loss of a loved one or the loss of a relationship that has been meaningful to us. In your case, your grief is for the loss of an emotionally secure, warm home environment in which you could grow in peace. That's not too much for any child to ask; in fact, it's normal. To have gone without it is to have lost a wonderful opportunity, and that is indeed something to grieve over. Now there's a difference between grief and self-pity. Self-pity seeks no resolution, no end to itself. People who are pitying themselves are usually intoxicated with the experience and the false consolation it provides. Grief is different, because it recognizes that something legitimate has been lost, that it is appropriate to feel some pain over that loss, and that eventually the person grieving will go on with life. Jesus grieved over Jerusalem, weeping over His people's unbelief and failure to recognize the time of salvation when it came. Certainly He wasn't wallowing in self-pity. Rather, He was acknowledging a tragedy, and reacting to it emotionally. Grief, then, is the beginning of a larger process of healing. To grieve over something means to recognize it for what it is, to acknowledge and express the pain that comes with that recognition, and to realize that the time of grief is seasonal, not permanent.

Then you determine what it is you seek from others. What means the most to you? Approval? Security? Affection? What do you do to get these things from others? Let me illustrate a case history in which a counselee asked herself these questions and came up with some valuable answers.

Gretchen's mother had silently rejected her from day one. Gretchen never knew exactly why, but it was clear from childhood onward that Mom had no time for her and no interest in her personal life. Mom was sophisticated and quite beautiful, a model homemaker who was popular and socially active. Gretchen was in awe of her mother, and longed for some sign that she was acceptable to her. But beyond the routine responsibilities that a mother has for a daughter, her mother never extended herself in any way to her. No hugging, no intimate talking, no play. So hungry was Gretchen for affection that at night she would deliberately throw her bedclothes off, then pretend to be sleeping, knowing that when Mom came to check on her she would have to rearrange the covers. As she did so, Gretchen could feel her mother's hands, if only for a moment, touching her and brushing against her. That was her main source of maternal touch.

Utterly devoid of female bonding, she felt no right to be feminine, no right to participate in women's activities. It's not that these activities were distasteful to her—she wasn't the proverbial "tomboy"—it's just that she had no confidence in herself as a girl and felt that other girls would never accept her. If Mom didn't like her, why would any woman? She became a loner, comforting herself with long walks and extended daydreams.

Dad, meanwhile, kept the entire family at arm's distance. He had insisted that his wife abandon her career as an artist and devote herself full-time to his comfort. This Gretchen's mother did, but not without clear resentment. Gretchen picked up on this resentment and absorbed it, disliking her father for making Mom so unhappy. "If she would only give me the chance," she told herself, "I could really please her."

But all hopes for that chance were dashed when, shortly before Gretchen's fourteenth birthday, her mother took her own life. No explanation, no goodbyes, only a brief note—the ultimate abandonment. Her father's way of handling the situation only worsened things. "Here's a note from your mother," he told Gretchen casually after learning of his wife's death. "She killed herself." With that he dropped the note into Gretchen's lap, turned, and left the room. Alone, as usual, Gretchen learned of her mother's suicide. And alone, as always, she cried.

She was learning many things. One, Mom never loved her and it was her own fault. Something was very, very unacceptable about her. Two, men were of no help whatsoever. Look at Dad, and his indifference to everyone, his selfishness. Three, people in general just aren't safe. You can't depend on them, you never know when they're going to leave, and you're better off not getting too involved with them.

Gretchen was wise enough to seek help later in life. She came to me a broken, lonely woman who had been involved in several brief, sexual relationships with both men and women, all nonintimate, some abusive. She had indeed played out her early beliefs by choosing people who would either neglect her or mistreat her, just as Mom and Dad did.

But she wanted to change. She began by coming to grips with the terrible pain her mother must have experienced, and the failure of both her parents to do anything constructive about their unhappiness. She drew courage and admitted that they were to blame for their mishandling of their daughter. And she stopped blaming herself for not being able to make them love her more. She recognized their limitations and their own personal battles. And in so doing, she learned to weep and grieve over what she never had, but should have had, as a little girl.

Her grief was powerful, but seasonal. Eventually she realized that, if her parents really were not average but had special problems, then they couldn't be accurate representatives of all men and women. And so she began to give people a chance again. She knew how badly she craved affection, and she didn't reprimand herself for that need. But she also knew that nobody could give her all the "strokes" she craved. She accepted that fact and took from people the love and friendship they had to offer. She tolerated their limitations, and found herself more comfortable with both sexes. She is still not inclined to date, and still holds some attraction toward women (though they are considerably weaker than in the past), but she is slowly rebuilding her identity as a woman. She now feels, as she puts it, like "one of the gals." That's a very good start.

How about you? Are you ready to challenge your old notions about yourself? Start by identifying what you've been looking for in lesbian relationships. You will find that it is available to you in nonsexual, healthy relationships as well. If you're ready to give such relationships a chance, I challenge you to seek them out. Through them you'll discover, perhaps for the first time, how much you have to offer and how lovable you really are.

12

Emotional Dependency and Lesbianism

by Dr. Carol Ahrens, Ph.D.

When Christian men deal with their homosexuality, they are frequently challenged to withdraw from sexual activity with other men. For many of them that presents a major difficulty. Sexual temptations beset them, and they experience a real pull toward erotic gratification. With women, however, I have found that sexual sin is rather easily abandoned. That's not to say that women are inherently nonsexual beings, devoid of sensual longings and even lustful thoughts. Rather, I have found that my counselees are able to give up lesbian sexual activity more easily than men are able to give up homosexual contacts, because their primary gratification in relationships with women has been of an emotional nature, not a sexual one. Their biggest challenge has been to deal with their emotional dependency.

What exactly is emotional dependency? What are its symptoms, its causes? And why is it so often linked with lesbianism? These are some of the questions I want to address in this chapter.

Emotional dependency is a state in which a woman feels totally reliant on another woman for safety and functioning. I'm not talking about the normal need we all have for close friendship and intimacy. I'm talking about a virtual obsession with another woman, one that leaves you hooked on her as surely as though you were hooked on a drug. When a woman is emotionally dependent, she feels as though she literally cannot exist without the object of her dependency. She needs constant reassurance from the other woman, consistent displays of affection, and large quantities of time with her. In short, emotional dependency is a bit like idolatry: Another person, in this case a woman, has become a sort of god.

When counselees in this position come to me saying they want to abandon lesbianism, they often say they'll give up the immoral sexual contact with the other person, but they can't imagine giving up the other person herself. They feel they must retain a close relationship with her, and will go through all sorts of bargaining and rationalizing to prove that it's perfectly O.K. to keep the relationship alive. "We'll keep it nonsexual," they usually say, "and we'll just be good friends." That sounds great, but too often it proves to be a stumbling block to any further growth. That's because the issue isn't just sex. It's unhealthy dependence on another woman which keeps the counselee from ever becoming her own person.

I'd be surprised if this hasn't been a part of your experience, because I see it so often. To fully understand emotional dependency in general (and yours in particular) we need to look at the origins of this problem.

Roots of Dependency

We all begin life in a state of total dependency. As infants we were dependent on our mothers and fathers for food, physical safety, and protection. Our emotional needs, too, sought fulfillment from these sources. We needed soothing, comforting, and nurturing. At that age we couldn't provide these things for ourselves, so we relied on other sources to provide them.

In time, though, healthy development requires more independence. Our parents' task was to slowly wean us from one dependent stage to another of less dependence. Nursing is a good example. Children are slowly weaned from the breast to the bottle, from the bottle to baby food, from baby food to solid food. Emotionally, too, such weaning should take place. Parents cuddle their children incessantly during the early years, but gradually they hold them less and allow them to move about more freely on their own. Some physical affection remains, of course, but in a healthy family the cuddling becomes less intense, replaced by more sophisticated means of communicating love, such as conversation and play. There would indeed be something wrong with a family in which the parents continued to carry their teenage children around in their arms saying "Cootchy-cootchy-coo!"

Independence comes when we have received enough affection and reassurance to build our confidence, and so we begin to depend less on others to care for us and we learn to take care of ourselves. *Whenever I see a woman who is emotionally dependent on another woman, I know that she has not been able to successfully complete this process of independence.*

Now there's nothing wrong with being needy, especially when we're very young. We were designed to need *affirmation*—that wonderful grace that our mothers bestow on us making us feel important and special. We need maternal recognition and gentleness. When we get it, we feel secure and able to become independent adult women. Unfortunately, we don't always get what we need.

Remember the problems of abandonment I mentioned in the previous chapter? Unhealthy dependency in adulthood is often the consequence of early abandonment. As always, we can't be sure who's to bless and who's to blame. After all, some mothers felt they really were giving their daughters plenty of time and affection, but for the daughter it may not have been enough. Or perhaps the mother had such serious problems of her own that she had no idea how to give love to her child. We can come up with plenty of reasons for a mother's limitations, but the fact remains that often she was unwilling or unable to make her daughter feel secure and cherished. The child may physically grow into adulthood, but psychologically she remains a needy, love-hungry little girl.

You might be one of those little girls in a woman's body. You may have become quite adept at hiding it, possibly ashamed of the intensity of your hunger for a mother's love. I've known dependent women who were outwardly impressive, competent in business, and high achievers in all areas. In fact, you may have learned to satisfy some of your needs by getting the acclaim that comes through achievement. Your vulnerability may frighten you, causing you to seek safety by appearing completely "together." Women in such cases are often great leaders and nurturers themselves, looked up to by others as a model of strength. But the need for mothering remains nevertheless—dormant, silent, and unfulfilled.

That's why many women fall into dependent relationships without knowing what's really happening to them. They can go for years without closeness, then suddenly they meet someone who taps into their deepest longings. It begins innocently enough, appearing to be nothing more than a nice friendship. Gradually, though, the friendship becomes a snare. Both parties become more reliant on the relationship, giving it priority over everything else. They call it a "special friendship" (sometimes even believing that it's a godsend), one that is unlike any they've had before. They've finally met somebody who makes them feel wonderfully loved, totally satisfied. Other friendships pale in comparison, and soon all socializing centers around this one person, this great companion, this emotional idol. And, as idols do, this person begins to hold tremendous power. Her approval is everything, her absence is intolerable. Everything in life revolves around her. Is it any wonder that such relationships become sexual? Some women who have never had a conscious lesbian attraction in their life suddenly find themselves sexually involved with a woman they thought was just a "good friend." They are shocked at their own situation, but are unwilling to leave it.

Symptoms of Dependency

How can you tell if this applies to you? There are several symptoms. One is an intense preoccupation with the other person. The Dependent Woman loses her sense of herself through total immersion in the Object of Dependence—the other woman. She doesn't seem to know where she stops and the other person begins. Boundaries are blurred, and fusion seems to have taken place. Like an emotional Siamese twin, she feels attached to her idol. This isn't love, although love may be present. It's obsession. And it's bondage. Common statements from such women include, "I need to know where she is every minute," "I feel completely thrown off when she doesn't call me," or "My whole body aches when I can't be with her."

Jealousy is another symptom. The Emotionally Dependent Woman needs to be the exclusive love of the other woman's life. Any other friendships seem threatening and any other sources of fulfillment for the other woman are seen as competition. And so the Dependent Woman tries to become the other's sole source of companionship and pleasure. She tries to become indispensable, thinking that if only she can meet her friend's needs perfectly and exquisitely, her friend will want no one else but her. The thought of the other woman dating or enjoying anybody else registers panic and a fear of abandonment.

And finally, the inability to make decisions or take actions without the other person's approval is a classic symptom of emotional dependency. In such relationships all plans must be checked out with the other person: Where to live, when to take a vacation, what to wear, and where to work are all subject to the other's scrutiny. Every detail of every decision is painstakingly worked out for fear of disapproval from the other party. The emotionally dependent relationship can be like a nonsexual marriage. Sometimes it's even more binding than that. I've known women who have had to call each other at work several times a day just because they could only function for so many hours without hearing each other's voice!

Each of these symptoms represents an inability to function without the person you're dependent on. The danger of this lies not only in its sinfully idolatrous nature, but in its binding nature as well. You cannot be all you're intended to be as long as you're held back by emotionally dependency. That's why God hates this particular sin: It restricts you from the best He has to offer.

I'm reminded of one of my own childhood scenes. My sister Betty, who is one year younger than I, was sitting behind me on a roller coaster. I had insisted on sitting in the first car in front of her, assuming the "brave" position. I was nervous, to be sure, but I was accustomed to being the strong one in the family and was playing that role to the hilt in this case.

Anyway, this particular ride was quite rickety and very high, and it felt as though it would collapse under its own weight any minute. Each seat had its own "security bar" for passengers to hang onto, but for some reason Betty decided that my neck would offer her more safety than the security bar. So instead of holding onto it, she held onto me. Every time we plunged down a hill or turned a corner, our bottoms flew off the seat. As if that weren't scary enough, Betty's hands, which clutched my throat throughout the ride, were nearly choking the life out of me! I wanted to let go of my own safety bar and wrench her little mitts off my neck, but I was too terrified to even move. I was gasping for air and turning red from her stranglehold, but she refused to release me. It was, to say the least, a real thrill ride.

Emotional dependency is like that. If you feel you've found someone who will give you all the love and security you've always wanted, you'll tend to clutch her as she'll clutch you, and both of you will strangle the very life out of each other.

There's nothing wrong with intense same-sex friendships. In fact I, like Joe, often see them as a major source of healing for the homosexual. But in emotionally dependent relationships there does not exist the healthy interaction of two people contributing to each other's lives. Instead, there exists two little girls trying to be to each other what they cannot be: a perfect mother. Until both parties recognize this, they will most likely continue this unhealthy, restricting way of relating.

Resolution

If you are involved in an emotionally dependent relationship, you need to withdraw from it. Nobody wants to hear that, and I understand why. These relationships are so intense, so overwhelming, so satisfying! But they are also deadly. You'll never mature as long as you stay in one. And so you need to come to some kind of resolution.

Resolution begins with recognition. Recognition is a mental act, not an emotional one. I point this out because your mind will acknowledge the need to withdraw from this relationship long before your emotions will follow suit. That's O.K. Our emotions usually do lag behind our mental processes. So start by recognizing the bind you're in, and make a conscious decision to disengage yourself from it. You'll be tempted to negotiate this decision by perhaps telling yourself you can keep seeing this person a little less often, call each other occasionally, and still remain friends. But experience has shown this to be impossible, because you're accustomed to very intense, intimate relating with your friend, and chances are you'll fall back into the old patterns if you give yourself a chance to. A clean break is necessary.

Once you've decided to make that break, let the person you're involved with know about your decision. This is hard and emotionally draining, but also necessary. You need to reach an agreement with her that, for a season, you'll need to stay separate. Explain why; don't just bolt and run. Let her know that your relationship with her is too intense and too binding, and that your dependency on her prevents your growth rather than enhancing it. Take responsibility for your part in this; don't blame her. There's no point in pretending the relationship hasn't been meaningful to you, so let her know that. But keep your commitment—don't let it go on. Make this a formal time for saying goodbye and wishing her God's best. Hopefully she will respect your decision. If not, you'll need to stand firm. This is the hardest part. Once you've gotten through it, you'll be well on your way to recovery.

Don't expect the next phase to be easy. Leaving a relationship like this can be like withdrawal, or the death of a loved one. So give yourself permission to grieve over this, and to feel the sadness of loss. The grief won't last forever. Be sure you don't frustrate the process by trying to hold onto her or by repressing the pain of losing her. Let it flow like tears, because tears are eventually expended.

When you've put some distance between yourself and the person you've been dependent on, you'll begin to see how unhealthy the relationship really was. Just as lovers often have such stars in their eyes that they cannot really see what their loved one is like, so people caught in emotional dependency tend to idealize their partner beyond all reason. Since this woman has been to you the source of all fulfillment, you have probably endowed her with a thousand wonderful qualities she never really had. With time, you'll begin to see her as less perfect and more human.

Don't assume that I'm saying you should eventually think she's a creep. You shouldn't (unless of course she really is a creep!). I'm only saying that you will most likely see her more realistically as time passes, and that this realism will bring an honest appraisal of her good and bad qualities. She will become, in your eyes, less of a goddess and more of a human. When this happens, you can be sure your healing is well underway.

Look at what you've given up in the meantime. While in the throes of emotional dependency, how many other friendships did you neglect? How many other activities did you avoid? These relationships tend to be quite exclusive, blocking out many opportunities. So now's the time to rebuild, to rekindle other friendships and start new ones. As you do so, realize something about yourself: You've tended to invest all your emotions into one intense, intimate relationship rather than investing in other friendships. Emotions can be like money—it's best not to put them all in one basket. I have found that dependent women prefer close-binding, one-on-one relationships and shy away from less-focused, more-casual ones. Yet we need more than one friend. We need close friends and acquaintances as well, so begin building your support system with both. You'll find that many other people can meet the needs you've expected one person to fill. In the long run, that makes for a safer and saner emotional state.

You don't want to repeat past mistakes, so look for the patterns of emotional dependency if and when they start to crop up again. Keep a healthy balance in your life, devoting time and energy to a variety of friendships. No one person can satisfy all your needs; that's too much to ask of anyone. So be a wise investor. You'll reap bountiful profits in the end.

PART FIVE

The Struggle for Identity

13

Dating and Marriage

*Then happy, I, that love and am beloved, Where I
may not remove, nor be removed.*

—William Shakespeare

Y ou began this process needing sexual romantic
fulfillment. Along the way we've discussed nonsexual intimacy, emotional needs which have been sexualized, and the need to discipline yourself to resist sexual
immorality, all of which are vital. But your goal has
been sexual wholeness, not nonsexuality. You remain a
sexual being, most likely needing erotic pleasure and
committed bonding. That's as it should be. Sex is something to be revered, celebrated, and thoroughly enjoyed.
I hope that as we've looked at the variety of ways sex can
be misused, you haven't developed an "anti-sex" attitude. Such an attitude is often the sad result of sexual
struggles—some people try, when resisting sexual sin,
to cut themselves off from sexuality altogether!

Physical and emotional intimacy with one person is
still a primary need for most of us. I've not yet known a
Fighter who, during the growth process, lost his or her

sex drive or desire for committed partnership. Additionally, most of us want a family life. That, too, is a desirable option for the majority.

But marriage is not the Promised Land. It is by no means a cure for sexual problems, nor will it in any way produce heterosexual response. Neither is it proof of a changed sexual orientation. After all, many homosexually oriented people are married. They retain a primary attraction to their own sex with minimal or no sexual attraction to their spouse. So from the start let's not view marriage as a goal or an indication that anything in particular has been achieved. After all, anyone can get married.

This needs to be stressed because too many Christians assume they *should* be married, that somehow they're second-rate or incomplete without a partner. Fighters, especially, are prone to view marriage as the ultimate goal which will validate their healing and put a seal on their heterosexuality. But nothing could be less true; marriage was never meant to be therapy or "proof of a cure."

It goes without saying, too, that marriage is never guaranteed; not to you, not to any single person. A number of factors come into play: meeting the right person, being ready for marital commitment, having the resources to establish a household. So bear in mind that your readiness for a mate is no guarantee that a mate will be found for or by you. If you're single, you're in the same position as all singles: You rely, ultimately, on God's sovereign timing.

Let me suggest you do two seemingly contradictory things: Consider marriage a possibility, but don't go out *looking* for a husband or wife. For that matter, don't regard marriage as a goal to be pursued. It may be something you desire, but if you pursue marriage for marriage's sake, you'll set yourself up for a premature commitment to the wrong person. Be about the business of living, relating, and working, and your chances of developing a committed relationship will be improved.

Dating: A Second Adolescence

If you're living a healthy lifestyle—fellowshipping, working, and socializing with members of both sexes— you'll be interacting with a number of people. Casual friendships with the opposite sex will usually develop, and at some point you might find yourself attracted to one person in particular. Van Den Aardweg describes the emergence of heterosexual attractions as follows:

> Mostly, the first heterosexual interests come rather unexpectedly, e.g. in the imagination, or upon seeing someone on the street. The first heterosexual infatuations may bear the marks of adolescence, as if the normal psychological growth process is rapidly being replicated. The client... discovers the existence of a sex divergent from his own... the male client eventually feels the enchantment of the female creature, her tender bodily forms and grace stir him erotically... the woman discovers excitement at the idea of being "possessed" and desired by the man.[1]

Of course, heterosexual attractions aren't proof that you've found Mr. or Miss Right. Attractions are nice to have, exciting if they are relatively new to you, but not enough to base a relationship on. There are more important things to consider before you begin dating someone.

Your mind, as Josh McDowell puts it, is your most important organ.[2] Before you start a romantic relationship, however casual, consider the qualities of the person you're attracted to, not just the attraction itself. Take your time, converse, and get to know each other. The question should never be, "Am I sexually attracted to this person?" but rather, "Is this a person I admire and would like to know better?"

That goes for anyone, regardless of his background. But it goes doubly for you because in your eagerness to experience heterosexual love you may jump into things too quickly. Don't jump the gun on romance; it will come when it's time. Caution and slow progress are the watchwords here.

When attraction and admiration for a person combine, you may want to spend more exclusive, prolonged time together. So go for it—why not?

But keep something in mind: You're probably not a kid, and neither is the person you're dating. Most Fighters are at least in their mid- to late twenties, often much older. That's because they've lived for awhile before addressing their homosexuality. You will probably be dating someone close to your age, and most people your age date rather seriously with an eye toward commitment. You may be experiencing an emotional adolescence, but when you date, there will be expectations more normally associated with adulthood. High school kids ask any number of people out to go steady without considering themselves "seriously involved" or engaged (at least not to the same degree as people your age). More simply put, the man or woman you date is probably looking for more than a good time—he or she is closer to setting down than a teenager might be. Keep that in mind. Even casual dating later in life carries expectations higher than adolescent dating. You need not consider your first date a prelude to the altar, but do consider the expectations the person you're dating may have.

Still, you should enjoy your "second adolescence." It combines the joys of young love with the freedom of adulthood—no curfews, no passing muster in front of your date's parents, no having to borrow the car. It's great! So be responsible, but enjoy.

If you begin seeing someone regularly, the issue of your past is going to cross your mind. Should the person you're dating know about your struggles with homosexuality? And if so, how early in the relationship should he or she be told?

While there are no set rules to follow, I strongly feel that the person you're becoming involved with has the right to know about your background early in the relationship. You might make the mistake of keeping it a secret because you're afraid of scaring a potential mate away before he or she gets to know you better. In my opinion, that's exactly why your partner has a right to know early on. Before she is emotionally invested in you, falling in love and hoping for marriage, she has a right to know what she's getting into, and to decide if she wants the relationship to continue.

That may seem unfair to you. After all, what's over is over. Aren't all things new, as Paul said? Yes, thank God, but getting to know someone means knowing significant things about that person's background. And, like it or not, your homosexuality has played a significant role in your emotional and social history. Far better to be up-front from the start than to be guilty of leading somebody on. And believe me, if you become seriously involved with someone and she discovers your background later in the relationship, she will feel betrayed and possibly mistrustful of you in the future. People don't like secrets, especially when they involve someone they're emotionally invested in.

There are also practical reasons for early disclosure. It's possible that your past involvement in homosexuality is known by others. Would you want to chance your boyfriend or girlfriend hearing about it from someone other than you? And what about any counseling or specialized ministry you're still involved with? Do you plan on keeping that a secret, too? That will mean cover-up and evasion, which are not the ingredients of a healthy relationship.

Besides, when you keep something important from someone you're getting close to, it interferes with your ability to fully enjoy that person. You'll feel the weight of secrecy and no small amount of anxiety. Yes, you may risk rejection by being honest from the start. But compared with the risk of sowing mistrust and disappointment in the long run, it's better to come clean at the beginning. Not necessarily on your first or second date, but at least before you let a dating relationship become steady and serious.

Courtship

You know when things are moving beyond casual dating. You start investing regular time in one person, your thoughts are consistently occupied with him or her, and the two of you take it for granted that you're "an item." You look forward to your time together, you share more about yourselves, you bond. You feel a genuine need to be with this one person who's now the object of your sexual attraction and emotional affections. Now's the time to ask yourself two hard questions.

"Have I found a best friend or a potential lover?"

Sadly, many Fighters find a man or woman they relate to so well, enjoy so much, and have such fun with that they mistake fondness for romantic interest. Of course, an element of friendship should exist in any steady relationship. Sometimes that's the only thing keeping it together when attractions and passion fluctuate. But be very honest with yourself. No wishful thinking, no premature declarations of "straight love, at last!" Is this a romantic friendship, or a friendship masquerading as romance?

If it's a friendship, there's nothing wrong with that. Just don't call it something else. Don't mislead yourself or anyone else. The quest for a normal woman-man bond leads people, often, to tell themselves they've found it before they really have, and the results can be destructive.

> *"Is my own life cleaned up enough so that I can shoulder the responsibility of a steady relationship?"*

A person whose life is out of control has no business being intimately involved with anyone else. If you're still sexually active, whether that means occasional backslides or habitual contacts, get your own act cleaned up before taking a courtship any further. Prove to your self that you can do that much before you presume to handle a serious relationship, because there's no way your activity won't interfere with and damage the person you're involved with.

I'm not saying, mind you, that sexual temptations of any kind disqualify you from dating or courting anyone. To be tempted is no sin; to habitually yield to temptation is proof you've got to get your act together.

Court Games

We all have little games we play with each other—rituals, ways of communicating, tendencies to avoid hard feelings. Games aren't necessarily good, but they're a reality. They appear most frequently when people start getting close, because closeness brings up our old insecurities and defenses. I believe we really want intimacy, but when it comes we respond in the funniest ways! To be intimate is to be vulnerable, to let somebody know us and all our little peculiarities. So we're a bit double-minded about intimacy. We crave it, but when it comes we react with what I call "games" because we're not sure how our partner will treat us once he or she really gets to know us.

Toward the beginning of any relationship we are interested in the other person thinking highly of us, so our best foot stays forward. As trust and affection build, we let the guard down and allow our partner to see a bit more of us. But we also want our partner to love us, or, specifically, we don't want our partner to *stop* loving us when she gets to know us better. And so the games begin.

Games are unique to the personalities of the people playing them, of course. But I'd like to look at two of them which I've seen repeated among Fighters and the people they're courting.

"Warning: You're Too Close to the Vehicle"

You've probably heard it by now—that spooking voice coming from a car you've innocently brushed past: "You're too close to the vehicle. Please step back." Apparently the auto is rigged with a very sensitive device which detects anyone getting "too close." The system warns you, in a none-too-friendly tone, that you've overstepped a certain boundary and there will be trouble if you don't back off.

Obviously this voice alarm is intended to prevent break-ins. But it can't tell what your intentions are when you approach the vehicle. You might just be walking past it with no intention of stopping. You might just be stepping close to admire the make of the car. Or you might simply be getting into your own car which is parked next to the Talking Turbo.

But alarms are not exclusively vocal, and they're not limited to autos. We carry them as well. We know when people are getting close—maybe "too close for comfort"— and we react, sometimes sending out unfriendly warning signals without knowing it.

The deepest pain we've felt has been caused by people we've been vulnerable to. We learn early in life that intimacy can be dangerous, that when we enjoy the luxury of closeness, we also take the chance of being wounded by the people we've opened ourselves up to. That teaches most of us to be reasonably cautious, and I suppose that's good. Even Jesus warned us against casting our pearls before swine—that is, we shouldn't give what is precious (including our feelings) to people who will misuse or abuse our gift.

But you may well have experienced more than your share of wounds. By the time you begin a courtship, it may have been years since you've allowed anyone to really know you. And it may have been even longer since you've allowed yourself to truly need another person. When you notice the development of real intimacy, then, you may start reacting with apprehension and even defensiveness. "Watch it," your alarm system says, "this person is getting too close! Remember what happened last time you let somebody into your heart?"

Besides past, hurtful episodes, you may also still be viewing yourself as an essentially unlovable person. Years of being on the "outside" of a rejecting, hostile society may have taught you that you're unusually defective, that if someone really sees inside you, they'll abandon you. You don't want that, so you protect yourself against too much closeness, too much self-disclosure. Feeling threatened by imminent rejection, you periodically withdraw.

Your poor partner, though, hasn't the slightest idea what's going on. All she knows is that you're suddenly closed, quiet, moody. She wonders what she's done wrong—something she said, perhaps? And so begins the age-old dialogue between the people afraid of intimacy and the people who want intimacy with them:

"You're very quiet tonight. Is something wrong?"

"Nothing. Everything's fine." (Translation: "We're getting awfully close here—I think you're starting to pick up on my little oddities and you're about to abandon me so I'm protecting myself defensively!")

"Your tone of voice doesn't sound all that fine to me. Is it something I've said?"

(Oh-oh, now I've started something.) "No, I'm just a little tired."

"I really think you're keeping something from me. Come on, what is it?"

(Aha! Rejection's coming any minute now, I can tell. She's probing me, she'll criticize me for being so sensitive, I just know it! Who does she think she is, anyway?)

"No, I said nothing's wrong! I just need some space. Let's call it a night."

Nice going.

You can keep this cycle up indefinitely, or you can choose to openly and honestly talk about your fears. Now is the time to grow up a bit. Admit that closeness is hard for you, that you're afraid of what your partner's going to see as you get to know each other better, and that, irrational as it may be, it makes you want to close yourself off. That's the only way you'll learn that you aren't so freakish, that someone else can know you without damaging you. That alone can bond you and the person you're courting in a relationship that's fuller and safer than ever.

"Let's Play Doctor"

Fighters can be a terribly introspective bunch, as can anyone who has gone through therapy or an intense growth process. Like students in their first years of clinical training, they talk incessantly about "issues," "recovery," and the "inner dynamics inherent in every interaction."

Too much "heavy talk" is in some cases just another convenient way of avoiding closeness. Instead of *being* close, some people forever *talk* about intimacy, examining it from every angle but never experiencing it. Common, too, is the tendency of people who've dealt with important personal matters to talk only about "The Really Big Issues of Life." When conversing, they seem to be saying, "Let's play doctor." The result is pop-therapy instead of an enjoyable, satisfying courtship.

You know you're playing doctor when you can't watch a movie together without psychoanalyzing the leading man. Or when you're more inclined to "explore the issues" in your relationship than to enjoy it. Or when you can't neck without discussing the rationale behind Touch Therapy.

I'm leery of anyone who throws out too much jargon, whether it's religious or psychological. The Christian who is forever saying "Praise the Lord" and punctuates every sentence with "Brother" or "Sister" sounds a bit phony to me—I usually assume he's trying too hard to convince me he's spiritual. Likewise, the person who is forever analyzing people and things may himself be hiding behind the Doctor Role. I usually feel like asking, "What don't you want me to know about you?"

Ask yourself if you're getting too analytical, too heavy, too serious. Courtship, after all, isn't therapy. And while there's certainly a time to be deep and inward, there's also a time for playfulness, laughter, and even a bit of silliness. See to it that these, too, are a part of your relationship.

The Marriage Question

Eventually, if you're seriously involved, you'll consider marriage. Aside from all the important matters to weigh before you make this decision, let me offer two more questions you should pose to yourself.

"Have I really left home?"

Both the Old and New Testament stress the importance of growing up and "leaving home" before marrying. The phrase "therefore shall a man leave his father and mother and cleave to his wife" does not imply any disrespect to the parents. It only means the wife or husband you choose must now become the priority in your life above all others.

Before going any further, then, determine whether or not the bonds between you and your parents are healthy. To be ready to leave home, a person not only has to be reasonably independent of parental influences. He or she also needs to have resolved any unfinished business with parents.

Unfinished business—conflicts in your family that have never been resolved or even addressed—will carry over into your marriage. They will affect your ability to fulfill the role of a spouse, and will eventually damage your spouse's relationship with both you and your parents. So before entering into a new family life, be sure your existing one is, as much as possible, free of long-held bitterness or misunderstandings.

"Have I proven my ability to be sexually responsible by maintaining sexual integrity for a significant period of time?"

You've been striving to maintain sexual integrity. Have you been successful? Is your private life the sort that would stand up to public scrutiny? If you've been unable, thus far, to abstain from sexual immorality, there's no reason to believe that marriage will in any way solve the problem. It will, in fact, add to it. Not only will your sex life remain out of control, but another innocent party will be brought into your immorality and, count on it, your spouse will be damaged by it.

So if you haven't proven to yourself that you are in control of your behavior, delay marriage. Don't even think of taking on the responsibility of managing a household until you've shown you can handle the responsibility of managing yourself.

Part of that responsibility will mean taking precautions. Specifically, if you haven't been tested for the AIDS virus, and you have been sexually active during your adult life, get tested. More than once, preferably. There's no excuse for entering into marriage with any doubts about your health, or with the possibility of endangering your loved ones. No matter how anxiety-provoking the thought may be to you, you've got to resolve this before you consummate your marriage. To do otherwise is immoral and reckless.

Sexual Preparation

When you consider the importance of the sexual relationship between wife and husband, it makes no sense not to plan for it. This intimate privilege, that distinguishes the transition from courtship to marriage, deserves more time, discussion, and preparation than any aspect of the wedding ceremony, because it will continue to be a part of your life long after the reception is over and the musicians have been paid.

Fighters usually approach their wedding night with nervous anticipation, much like any newlywed couple but with special concerns. For men, the desire to sexually bond is often accompanied by performance anxiety. This may be the first time the groom has had intercourse with a woman. He worries about his ability to perform, to give to his bride pleasure, to block out past sexual experiences and thoroughly enjoy his wedding night. The bride may have had very unsatisfactory sexual relationships with men in the past—will it be any better this time? What's expected of her? Will she be treated with respect and gentleness?

Talking diffuses these fears and relieves the anxiety these questions bring up. So at this point, you should be openly discussing whatever qualms or questions you have about your wedding night. If you have insecurities, talk them out together. If there are specific fears you have about the sex act, name them and ask for your partner's feedback and reassurance. That sort of honesty will go far toward maximizing your sexual pleasure.

Keep in mind, too, the fact that your wedding night is not the one and only time you'll be sexually involved. You've got the rest of your married life to enjoy each other! So determine from the start that when you come together it will be for mutual enjoyment and closeness, not just intercourse. Your wedding night is a time to make love, to seek maximum pleasure for your partner and express yourself in ways you've been unable to up till now. Keep the sexual relationship in that perspective and you'll find it a source of intense fulfillment.

Marriage is not the answer to the struggle for sexual identity. In many ways it opens up more struggles, because being a husband or a wife requires you to learn, daily, about your personhood, your weakness, your sexuality. Being a woman with a man, or a man with a woman, redefines the experience of masculinity and femininity. It is an ongoing process of individual and mutual discover, a permanent struggle to fulfill the most responsible role you can take on.

But what a joyous struggle it is! God's best to you as you enter it.

14

Having Done All, Stand

*Wherefore take unto you the whole armor of God,
that ye may be able to stand in the evil day, and having
done all, to stand.*

—Ephesians 6:13

The struggle for sexual identity is answered not by becoming sexually perfected, but by becoming sexually mature. And a mature sexual identity is born of a mature self-perception.

You are not simply a homosexual, heterosexual, ex-gay, or whatever. You are a child of God, bearing His image and indwelt by His Spirit. You have imperfections in all aspects of life, but they do not define you, nor do they rule you. If they exist, they exist as minor nuisances, not major bondages.

Your sexual identity has been clarified as you have begun to understand what factors combined to make up your sexual history, your struggles, your needs. In understanding these factors you've lost the confusion you held for so long about why you retained erotic desire you never asked for or chose. Along with that understanding came a healthy sense of absolution—you no longer held yourself in contempt for having homosexual desires, although you assumed full responsibility for what you'd done with them.

And with that understanding came acceptance. Acceptance is not approval, but a calm realization that there are parts of life you cannot change, including your past, your wounds, your present struggles. You work on them, to be sure, because your identity as a child of God gives you a hunger for freedom from any sort of bondage. But you don't worry about them. They've lost their control over you, including their ability to bring stress and sadness into your life.

With a mature sexual identity comes a commitment to conform your behavior and expression of all kinds, sexual and nonsexual, to God's standards. Having experienced the impact of His Spirit on your sexuality, you want nothing less than the best He has for you. And you've learned that the discipline He requires of you is enforced to insure that you do indeed experience nothing less than the best. With that knowledge comes assurance and, at long last, peace.

There's little left to say; a few quick thoughts, though may be in order.

Don't ever say you've arrived. You, like all of us, will continue to struggle against any number of temptations and tendencies as long as you're alive and kicking. So even if you are completely free of any homosexual tendencies, there's a myriad of other issues to deal with. Nothing but your death or the coming of Christ will change that.

Besides, you've no guarantee that you're immune to homosexual struggles. If they are completely gone, wonderful. But who is to say they'll never return? Don't get too confident—that's always a sign of danger. Maintain your integrity as though it's always in danger of being compromised because, in fact, it is. Remember Paul's warning: "Let him who thinks he stands take heed lest he fall (1 Corinthians 10:12).

Don't jump into the world of ministry or testimony. Many a Fighter has mistakenly assumed he's called to "ex-gay ministry" just because of the process he's gone through. That's a mistake—your calling in life may have nothing to do with homosexuality and healing. So don't limit your future options because of your past. If you're called to that sort of work, you'll know it. If you feel no special inclination toward it, then let the dead past remain dead.

Above everything else, be grateful, humble, aware of the Lord your God who brought you out of slippery places and set you on a rock. It was He, not you, who created in your heart a dissatisfaction with homosexuality. He disengaged you from habits and tendencies that were destructive. No matter how hard you have striven to learn, to repent, and to grow, it has been His grace that has enabled you do to so. Without it, you would never have made it this far. Glory in the new life you have, by all means. But never forget who gave it to you. Never forget where you are now, and where, but for His intervention, you might have been.

PART SIX

The Other Struggle

15

To Parents: Love and Let Go

In the film *Steel Magnolias* a young man approaches his parents with a terrible announcement:

> "Mom, Dad, I want to tell you I have terminal brain cancer."
> Shock, terror.
> "Just kidding, I'm fine. But I do want to tell you I'm gay."

There's a unique way to come out of the closet! And while an approach like that leaves a bit to be desired, it does express the dilemma families face when confronted with a son's or daughter's homosexuality. The offspring realize, in most cases, that news of their sexual preference will create an upheaval in the home and that there will usually be a stunned reaction from the parents.

Author Barbara Johnson knows the situation all too well. In her book *Where Does a Mother Go to Resign?*

(Bethany House, 1979) she relates the anguish she felt when she discovered her son's homosexuality:

> Flashing in my mind was this wonderful son who was so bubbly and happy—such a joy to have around. Thinking of him entwined with some other male brought heaves of heavy sobbing from deep wounds of agony.[1]

Her personal journey from shock to acceptance and a willingness to release her son to God and his own choices makes for compelling (and often humorous) reading. So right off the bat, if you're a parent reading this out of concern for your son or daughter, I suggest you get a copy of Johnson's book. For many people, it's been an emotional lifesaver.

She makes a good point about reaction, one which is the foundation of her ministry, which is known as "Spatula Ministries." She says that when parents hear about a son or daughter's homosexuality, they need a spatula to scrape them off the ceiling. But coming off the ceiling is just the beginning—when a loved one's orientation is homosexual, families are challenged and stretched.

How a family responds to the issue will have much to do with what the issue really is. Is the homosexually oriented family member comfortable with homosexuality? Does he want help? Has he decided to be openly gay? Is he or she a Christian? These are all questions that help determine how the issue should be approached. In this chapter, I'd like to look at the most common situations that arise when homosexuality hits home, emphasizing what *not* to do as much as what one *should* be done.

"My adult son/daughter just told me he's/ she's gay. What can I do?"

This question is becoming more and more common. Almost half of the phone calls I receive are from parents wanting to know how they can deal with their adult children and, as always, the immediate family crisis hits the roots of deeper family issues. My advice usually follows these lines:

1. *Ascertain your son's or daughter's feelings about homosexuality.* Is he telling you he accepts it? Is he comfortable with it? Has he decided to identify himself with the gay community, or is he simply convinced that homosexuality is a permanent part of his makeup and that, even though he may not be openly gay, he's sure that he will always be that way? Or is he undecided?

These questions clarify what it is your child is really saying to you. He may be informing you that he's gay and that's it—he has no intention of changing. Or he may be asking you for help, as in "I think I'm gay and I don't want to be. What can I do?"

If homosexually oriented children say that they've accepted their homosexuality, they are probably asking you to accept it as well. And on the one hand, you must. You may never accept it as being normal or desirable, but you have no choice but to accept the fact that, to them, it is normal. You cannot change their minds; you cannot change their feelings no matter how much you'd like to. Likewise, you can't give your approval or blessing to it. The best you can do is accept their decision, and this will no doubt be your greatest challenge.

If they're asking you for help, by all means make yourself available to them. Help them seek out the counseling or ministry that will be suitable for them, and support them for having the integrity to face an issue—a tough one, at that—and deal with it honestly.

2. *Acknowledge the compliment they've paid you by being honest about themselves.* I know you're thinking, "Some compliment!" but it is one. By disclosing their

feelings to you they are trusting you with very personal, difficult information. They're really asking if they can be honest with you without fear of retaliation. (Remember that unless you discovered their orientation by accident, they really didn't have to tell you at all!) Acknowledgment does not imply tacit approval—you can appreciate a person's willingness to be open with you without telling them you approve of what they're being open about.

3. *Express your own feelings.* Few homosexually oriented sons or daughters expect their parents to just shrug the news off without a reaction, so be honest. Tell them how you feel—hurt, angry, frightened, disillusioned—without accusing them. It's one thing to say, "You make me sick! That's disgusting, and I can't stand the sight of you!" It's something else to say, "I feel shocked. I don't know how to take this. I'm really in pain." When expressing yourself, don't hedge on your own beliefs. It would be unreasonable for your son or daughter to expect you to approve of something just because he approves of it. So there's no reason to deny your beliefs or refrain from saying something such as, "Look, I can never believe that homosexuality is normal. That goes against all my principles." This again is different than the more alienating approach: "Don't you know that it's a perversion and you're gonna burn for it?"

4. *Listen.* Let your son or daughter explain to you how he or she reached this decision or understanding. Some parents are afraid to hear their children's experiences because they feel that if they don't preach and condemn, their willingness to listen might be taken for approval. That's not true. When Jesus approached the Samaritan woman in John's Gospel, He didn't even bring up the subject of her sex life, though He knew she'd had several men in the past and was living with a man who wasn't her husband. Yet we'd hardly take that to be approval on His part!

5. *State your own limitations.* Many parents are put on the defensive when their grown children insist that their gay lovers be allowed to spend the night in the family's home with them, or join the family during holiday gatherings. These are not decisions that you should be coerced into. You've got to decide what you are and are not comfortable with in your own home. This is not forcing your views on your son or daughter; it's just an insistence that you be allowed to decide these things for yourself. Just as you must respect your children's rights to live their lives as they see fit, so they must respect your right to do the same.

And these steps are just the beginning. You now have to deal with the new information you've been given— your son or daughter is gay. Now what? There are three special temptations parents in your position may fall into, temptations you'd do well to avoid.

You Didn't Do It

First, don't take responsibility for your child's sexual orientation. That may seem hard, even contradictory in light of some theories expressed in this book. But remember that even though family dynamics might have something to do with homosexual development, they cannot and do not cause it. Besides, you can't make another person homosexual any more than you can make another person heterosexual. In short, you didn't do this. You couldn't have, even if you'd tried.

That's not to say that if, while examining your own past, you see things you regret and want to discuss with your son or daughter, you shouldn't do so. There's nothing wrong with that. But resist the temptation of blaming yourself for the homosexuality you're now aware of. Take responsibility for what you have done; refuse responsibility for what you could never do.

Which brings to mind the question of parental responsibility in general. Is a child's problem in adulthood an indication of parental failures? No, definitely not. Adam and Eve, Isaac, Jacob, David—any number of biblical characters produced offspring that had problems later in life. It is the fallen nature, not parental shortcomings, which is ultimately the cause of all dysfunction, sin, and perversion. To assume responsibility for an adult child's sin is to assume a certain omnipotence. And clearly, whatever else we may be, parents are not omnipotent.

"I'll Fix It!"

A second common temptation is the urge to rescue our children. How many fathers and mothers have called me saying:

> "I'm bringing my son in for counseling because I want him fixed!"
> "Does your son want counseling?" I ask.
> "Not really, but I know he really needs it. We've got to take care of this boy!"

But "this boy" might now want to be "taken care of," and to force your good intentions on him will only alienate him in the long run, doing real damage to your relationship with him in the future. If and when he wants help, he'll seek if for himself. If he doesn't want it, all the counseling that money can buy won't accomplish a thing.

The urge to rescue our adult children is understandable. We spend years caring for them, protecting them, being their primary source of comfort and training. It's hard—maybe impossible—to relinquish caretaking instincts just because the children have grown up. But we have no choice.

You have to eventually release your children to God, their free choices, and the consequences of their own decisions. That's not to imply that you can ever stop caring, worrying, or grieving. But you can't rescue your children, you can't decide for them, you can't control them. Nor should you try.

"We're Finished"

The last temptation, which can lead to the worst sort of tragedies, is the temptation some parents feel to cut their children off. "If you want to be gay," they say, "then you can just stay out of my life!"

Why? Did your son or daughter stop being your offspring the moment you found out about his or her sexuality? And, more to the point, did you ever have an agreement with him that he'd live his life as you see fit or else you'd have nothing to do with him?

Cutting your flesh and blood off is a chilling thing to do, a decision you'll have to live with long after you've gotten over the shock of your son's or daughter's homosexuality.

Your child didn't change when he told you about his homosexuality. That's the same child you've known all these years. You only know more about him now. The question is: Can you continue to have a relationship with him with this newfound knowledge?

I believe you can. And, as much as possible, you should try. There are times when it is impossible, I know. Sometimes sons or daughters will have nothing to do with their families unless the family changes its views on homosexuality. That's an unfair, irrational thing to force on anyone. But if both you and your adult child can be clear on this point—we disagree on homosexuality but love each other and want to continue our relationship—then keep the door open. Shock and disappointment in a child's behavior will never sever the bonds existing between you and that child.

> *"How can I prevent my children from becoming homosexual?"*

There's no guarantee that if you follow certain guidelines your child will develop a normal sexual orientation. So in that sense, there's nothing you can do to prevent your child from becoming homosexual.[2]

The best way to minimize the possibility, though, is to raise your children exactly the way you should be raising them anyway: in a healthy, loving environment of respect, godliness, and support.

Fathers and sons need special times together, as do mothers and daughters. To neglect this is to open the door to any number of problems, homosexuality included. Likewise, relationships between child and parent of the opposite sex should be affirming, especially as the child is moving into adolescence and young adulthood. A father needs to affirm, not inhibit, his daughter's developing womanhood. She needs to know that her father regards her highly, praises her, and celebrates her. A son should be confident that his mother respects his young manhood, admiring it and approving of it. Again, to neglect these areas will create problems of some sort, sexual or otherwise, and to pay attention to them will minimize the risk of sexual difficulties in the future.

> *"I'm a single mother. Will my son have special problems by not having a father around?"*

No reason to assume that he will. Of course, a two-parent home is ideal, but many fine, healthy children are being raised in single-parent homes. Remember, the absence of a father is not necessarily traumatic to a boy. Far more traumatic is the presence of a father who seems disinterested or hostile.

If you're concerned, though, about a lack of male presence in your son's life, do what you can to provide him opportunities to interact with other boys and men. Group organizations are especially handy and good for this purpose.

But again, never assume the absence of a father guarantees problems, any more than the presence of a father guarantees emotional health.

> *"But I'm still in such pain over my son's/ daughter's homosexuality! Isn't there anything else I can do?"*

Yes. Take care of yourself. You can't change the situation, and you can't change someone else's mind, but you can get the help you need to deal with your own feelings.

Find someone to talk to. It can be a good friend, a counselor, or a pastor, as long as it's someone *whom you trust* and *who is removed enough from the situation to give objective, clear feedback*. You need to talk! If there is a group of parents in your situation who meet together, by all means join them (see "Spatula Ministries" in Resources). But whatever you do, don't keep this to yourself. Find an outlet for your feelings and a listening, sympathetic person to lean on.

Don't stop loving your children, but don't clutch them either. To let go of our children means to acknowledge our inability to change them, rescue them, "fix" them. They were only ours to train and protect for a season, and now the season is over. You still have your life, and to live it fully is at this point the most effective and reasonable thing to do.

16

To the Church: Conflict, Conviction, and Compassion

In this regard gay activists mirrored the passage of confrontation politics—the purpose of protest was no longer to make public a point of view, but rather to halt unacceptable practices—the traditional willingness to tolerate the views of one's opponents was discarded.

—Ronald Bayer, 1981

We stepped out of the auditorium single file, facing a crowd of gay activists holding candles, waving signs, and blowing whistles. Security guards had formed a narrow aisle for us to walk through, but there were still less than five feet between us and the protestors. Their banner identified them as "Queer Nation," their signs exhorted us to "Heal Ourselves," Stop the Violence," and a few other things unmentionable in this writing. Their faces were even more expressive than the slogans they repeated: "Stop the violence, stop the hate"; "Once queer, always queer"; "Sexist, racist, anti-gay, born-again bigots go away!"

Their hatred was louder than their shouting, more colorful than the expletives they were hurling at us. We were a sorry lot, we bigots; certainly we were no credit to the tradition of fascism that they accused us of carrying on. No self-respecting hatemongers would have conducted themselves the way we did. Few of us shouted back, none of us threw punches. Instead, without cue or prompting, we linked arms, faced the crowd, and began singing hymns. Some knelt and prayed on the spot, others tried vainly to engage the protestors in some reasonable dialogue. Most of us watched, refusing to avoid the ugly scene but also determined not to contribute to its ugliness. It was quite a way to cap off an evening of worship and teaching.

It was the 16th Annual Conference of Exodus International at the University of Toronto in Canada. This conference, held in a different location each year, provides Exodus leaders with a chance to meet and network with other ministry leaders; teach workshops on sexuality, relationships, and recovery; and meet with parties interested in our work. Most of us look forward to the week-long gathering. It is usually peaceful and provides a much-needed boost to our morale.

We'd already heard some rumblings of protest before the confrontation with Queer Nation. From the time we arrived in Canada, newspaper reports had carried quotes from gay leaders denouncing us and our view on homosexuality. That's nothing new—the quickest way to be the Bad Guy these days is to question the legitimacy of homosexuality and hold a traditional viewpoint on moral issues. But we were surprised at the lengths to which they had gone this year to harass and intimidate us.

So yes, we expected a little trouble. And no, nothing terrible happened. Intense and enlightening, but not terrible. As the confrontation continued that night, I spoke with a few of the activists. "Your presence here is oppressive to us," one of them informed me.

"But how," I asked, "is it oppressive to hold a different viewpoint? We're not forcing it on you; in fact, the way you live your life is your own business and I wouldn't interfere. But don't we have a right to offer whatever help we can to people who aren't satisfied being gay?"

"Well," he said, "we think your ideas are crazy and homophobic."

End of discussion; he walked away.

My ideas? Did I write the Bible? It occurred to me and several other people with whom I later spoke that our viewpoint, which is held by the majority of Christians, was what prompted the outrage. The protestors weren't reviling us; they were reviling the notion that homosexuality is abnormal, immoral, and a perversion of God's intention for sexual experience. As long as we—or anyone—hold such a view, there will be controversy. Our confrontation was a microcosm of what the church at large is about to face.

There are basically two ways we can respond to the confrontation: We can modify our beliefs or stand our ground. Many congregations are opting for the former, sacrificing biblical integrity in the name of compassion. That's tragic, and, as Chuck Smith of Calvary Chapel stated recently, "a sign of weakness within the church that it [the issue of whether homosexuality and Christianity are compatible] is even a topic of debate. It should not even be a question because the Bible is very clear on the subject."[1]

The second option is to stand our ground, refusing to be intimated by the growing number of voices clamoring for a revision of clear biblical teaching. But how we stand our ground is equally important. There we are faced with a seemingly impossible challenge: to express our convictions with reason and compassion. "To be really Bible-believing and true to our living Christ, each issue demands a balance which says 'no' to two opposite errors," says Francis Schaeffer. "We can neither compromise love in the name of holiness; nor can we compromise holiness in the name of love. Or to say it another way: the devil never gives us the luxury of fighting the battle on just one front."[2]

We can't duck the issue of homosexuality, but neither can we effectively address it unless our response is balanced. To take it a step further, not only will our response need to be balanced; it will need to recognize the individuality of the homosexually oriented person we're dealing with. Not all gays are activists. Some are activists, others are more moderate, and others are dissatisfied with their sexuality and want our help. Obviously our approach to these groups will have to vary. I'd like to look briefly, then, at the gay activist, the moderate, and the Fighter and offer some thoughts on a balanced, effective response to each.

The Church and the Activist

In *A Tale of Two Cities* Dickens described an uprising of people who had been pushed too far, oppressed for too long, victimized too horribly. The citizens of France had been ground underfoot by the Aristocrats, treated inhumanly and taxed without mercy by the upper-class tyrants. They brooded for years, planning the day they would take over and reverse the power structure. When the revolution came and their position of power over the Aristocrats was secured, they exacted vengeance without reason, blindly striking down anyone who opposed them and establishing a new form of terrorism that, to them, was really justice. They went into overkill, and though their initial grievances against their enemies were legitimate, their newly established system was every bit as tyrannical as the one they had overthrown. The oppressed were now the oppressors, lopping the heads off anyone who questioned them.

You can't look at the tactics and goals of gay activists without seeing the correlation. To begin with, they, too, have been frequently mistreated. And many of their complaints against the church and society are legitimate. Try to understand a bit of their background.

A Genesis of Rage

They never asked for their homosexual orientation. They had no control over whatever influences in early life contributed to it. They never chose to be attracted to their own sex; they only became aware, at some point, that those attractions existed.

Usually their awareness of their sexual feelings came as a vague realization that they were "different." That difference may have been noticeable to others (when boys are effeminate or girls "boyish"), or it may have been a private sense of feelings that other kids didn't seem to have. Most kids in this position are aware of homosexual feelings before they even know what homosexuality is. Sooner or later they hear the jokes about "queers." Not sure what a "queer" is, they assume only that, whatever it is, it's not a very popular thing to be. When it occurs to them that the definition of a "queer" or "fag" matches their sexual feelings, they are aware of their homosexuality, but they're also aware of the reaction they'd get from almost anyone they would disclose their orientation to. Their friends would ostracize them; their parents would be shocked, or devastated, or rejecting (or so they assume, and often they're absolutely right). And so begin the years of secrecy, hiding, self-loathing.

At first they assume or at least hope that, as time passes, they will outgrow their homosexuality. Often they pray hard and concentrate even harder, trying to change. And, sadly, they often assume that the problem is them—that something is fundamentally sick or evil about them to have these feelings. Their environment doesn't help much. By the time they've entered adolescence they know that to be gay is, in most teenage circles, one of the worst things one can be. This drives them further inward, more determined than ever to let no one in on their secret.

Of course, in some cases it's no secret at all. God help the teenage boy who's effeminate, the teenage girl with masculine traits. They are the objects of senseless cruelty, harassed and ridiculed at every turn by their peers. Yet even in the cases of adolescents whose homosexuality isn't obvious (they're the majority, by the way) there's an understanding that they, too, would be openly persecuted if their peers knew the whole truth.

Can you imagine, on top of the inward turmoil these kids experience, the rage that starts to build inside of them? They are isolated, lonely, and often abused by others who fear them or loathe them or both. The church tells them they're sinning and society (in general) tells them they're oddballs, yet no one tells them what to do about it! They're in pain, to be sure, but someday that pain will translate into anger.

At some point they consider the gay community—a community that will accept them as they are, made up of people like them who have experienced a similar emotional journey. They make a decision to "come out," to quit fighting their inclinations and accept them, and in many cases to advise friends and loved ones of their decision. The coming-out experience is exhilarating. Finally the secret's out; no more hiding, fearing, pretending. For most, it feels wonderful. And for those who are activists today, the decision to come out was probably accompanied by a commitment: "I will never allow anyone or any group to ever put me down, humiliate me, or oppress me in any way ever again!"

―――――

Most of the repenting that needs to be done on this issue of homosexuality needs to be done by straight people, including straight Christians. By far the greater sin in our church is the

*sin of neglect, fear, hatred, just wanting to
brush these people under the rug.*[3]

—Richard Lovelace, 1981

Add to these personal experiences the animosity
that's been growing between conservative Christians
and gays these past few decades. The burgeoning Gay
Rights movement of the late sixties and early seventies
begged some sort of Christian response. A natural result of the sexual revolution of the sixties, the Gay
Rights movement began to force itself on American
consciousness as gays began identifying themselves
without apology in larger numbers. No longer were they
asking for tolerance; they were demanding acceptance
for themselves and their sexuality. Unbeknownst to
most of us, they made tremendous political, educational,
and even religious inroads. (As early as 1969 some
denominations were quietly reconsidering their stand
on homosexuality.) Yet by and large, the church offered
little in the way of comment. Worse yet, virtually no
efforts were made to extend the gospel to these people.
Maybe we were afraid of the subject, or perhaps we were
intimidated by our own ignorance of it. At any rate, our
lack of compassion was marked by our failure to respond
to a huge, growing need in America.

Our response accelerated from silence to a deafening
roar in the mid to late seventies, beginning with what is
now considered a watershed event in the Gay Rights
movement—the Anita Bryant Crusade in Dade County,
Florida. In 1976, when Dade County passed an anti-
discrimination bill prohibiting discrimination in housing
or employment based on sexual orientation, Miss Bryant
took action. With the encouragement of her pastor and
supporters, she spearheaded a referendum which gained
national attention. Believing that legislation such as
that of Dade County was in fact highly discriminatory

toward those holding traditional moral values, she successfully campaigned to have the law repealed. Although the outcome of the Bryant campaign was favorable, the events occurring during the campaign itself would once and forever change the church's response toward homosexuality, a change that was, in many ways, not for the better.

Essentially, we seemed to rise up in unanimous protest against the notions that homosexuality should ever be considered normal and that homosexuals should be granted the same minority status afforded to race, sex, and religion. That protest was good in and of itself, but the way it was expressed was actually damaging in many cases. Remember, these were the early days of Christian television, when ministers were finding new avenues of influence through the airwaves. And so over the air our leaders began expressing strong views not only on homosexuality but on homosexuals themselves. And that is precisely where we erred.

Extravagant, ill-informed remarks about gays were hurled from the televangelists' studios. It wasn't enough to preach against the sin of homosexuality, we needed to underscore our point by degrading, in the public's eye, anyone who practiced it. With little concern for accuracy, we exploited the stereotype most Americans had of homosexuals—they were all promiscuous, they were all effeminate, they all practiced their vile deeds in public places and posed a serious threat to the safety of our children. We weren't always wrong, of course. Some homosexuals fit that description quite well. But far too many of them didn't, a fact we refused to realize. It was politically expedient to cast them all in the same mold, as if to allow that some of them were rather moderate citizens would have somehow weakened our argument against their habits and lifestyles.

Not only were irresponsible generalizations becoming commonplace, they were also being made with a certain degree of relish. We wanted, it seems, to believe the very worst about these people and encourage others to do the same. Even more disturbing was the lack of gospel invitation extended to the gays. At the very least, one would think that having spent time and energy denouncing them, we would have ended our rebukes with an explanation of the grace of God manifest in the cross. Instead, like Jonah preaching to the Ninevites, we really seemed to hate these people and care little for their salvation. We wanted them stopped, but we didn't want them saved. Or so it appeared.

We sent a strong message to the gay community in those days: "We'll fight you every stop of the way, and although we claim to "love" souls as Christ loves them, we don't care much for yours. What we do care about is your defeat, and that will be the focus of our efforts when we deal with you."

That is a message they will never forget.[4]

————————

*Jesus did not see disease as God's judgment
but as an opportunity to show God's glory and
mercy.*[5]

—Glenn Wood, M.D. and
John Dietric, M.D., 1990

If irresponsibility marked our public stance toward homosexuality in the seventies, we outdid ourselves in the eighties during the advent of the AIDS epidemic. Our hearts were unmoved when we saw pictures of emaciated young men crying in agonized confusion. They were beneath our compassion; instead, we pronounced (with smug satisfaction) the judgment of God upon the perverts of America. We seemed to feel they'd gotten what was coming to them and one would almost think we rejoiced in it. Preacher after preacher reminded his congregation that homosexuals were tasting God's wrath, and it was about time. We judged, we pontificated, we rambled.

But where was our compassion? We'd become adept at hard truth, but couldn't see that AIDS was affording us the greatest opportunity we'd ever had to finally reach the gay community with the gospel. Didn't it sink in that people were dying, alone and desperate, waiting to be harvested right before our eyes? Where were our missions, our visitation programs, our calls to action? *Did we really feel that the soul of a homosexual was of less value to God than the soul of a heterosexual?*

The greatest chance of a decade went up in smoke before our eyes. Our pronouncements of judgment did little good for these people. Doing good and showing mercy to them was relegated to the liberals, the New Agers, and the gays themselves. They filled the gap we should have bridged from the beginning. They stepped in with service programs, hospital visitation, and human comfort. While we pointed our fingers, the non-believers and the cults extended their hands. If the message we'd sent to the homosexual in the seventies was one of contempt, the message of the eighties was one of indifference, even in the face of death.

And so they perceived our response, accurately so in many instances, and they reciprocated. They returned our contempt twentyfold, considering us to be a community of cruel, twisted people. The hatred we felt from the Queer Nation protestors was, I believe, the fruit of our own mishandling of the homosexual issue.

You might well say, "But all Christians didn't blow it! Many of us really *did* care about AIDS patients and gays, and never meant them any harm." You may be right, but remember that the church, for better or worse, is represented by its most visible spokespersons. When they speak, those to whom they speak assume that they represent all of us. And so the anger many of them felt during their early years was fueled all the more by their perception of us, a perception that was not always inaccurate.

Maximum Overkill

But our errors will never justify the antics of the homosexual militants. Like the French citizens in Dickens' story, they've gone into overkill. In *Tale of Two Cities* the citizens forbade anyone to speak against their new order under threat of the guillotine. And gay activists, not content to allow anyone to speak against them or their goals, are equally open about their intolerance:

> Articles in *Outweek* [a gay publication] have backed taking away free speech from anyone alleged to be homophobic and have urged the use of violence against straight oppressors.[6]

The French citizens railed against the violence the Aristocrats had committed against them, yet they advocated mass violence against their former oppressors (and anyone they deemed an enemy of the republic) without apology or exceptions. So gay activists consider terrorism an acceptable method of achieving their ends and silencing their enemies:

> A recent cover [of *Outweek*] featured a lesbian pointing a gun at the reader, with the headline: "Taking aim at bashers!" [Presumably "gay bashers," which often means anyone who opposes homosexuality.] Another proclaimed, "We hate straights."[7]

The double standard here is nearly unbearable. Activists unanimously decry the violence committed against gays. In some cases they cite violent acts of gay bashing in which clearly disturbed people physically, randomly attack gays. This type of violence should be decried by all of us, and its perpetrators punished to full extent of the law. At other times, though, they consider verbal slurs to be acts of violence, acts which they themselves commit boldly and openly (and not against the people who directly attack them, by the way, but against those of us they've targeted as "homophobes"). And in some cases, they encourage the very sort of violence they condemn when it directed against them.

By the way of example, one of the best known AIDS activists in America is Larry Kramer, founder of the militant group ACT UP (AIDS Coalition to Unleash Power) which is the forerunner of other such groups. Kramer is on record as advocating violence and even murder:

> He [Kramer] then began the meeting with a soft spoken announcement that he wanted to set up a group to do target practice, to learn how to use guns against the police and gay-bashers.[8]

> Asked to be more precise, Kramer looks grim and says that "the new phase is terrorism...I don't know whether it means burning buildings, or killing people or setting fire to yourselves."[9]

> "I think, when I am ready to go," [referring to his health after learning he'd been exposed to the AIDS virus], "I'll take somebody with me."[10]

Many in the gay community disagree strongly with Kramer, and many would not back his call to violence. But think for a minute: If a Christian leader ever made such statements, would there be a major newspaper in

America that wouldn't splash his words on the front page? If Randall Terry, Jerry Falwell, or Phyllis Schlafly (all of whom are considered bigots and homophobes by the gay community) advocated any form of violence against gays, wouldn't there be a national outcry, and rightfully so? Yet somehow a nationally recognized leader in the gay community can publicly encourage murder without impunity. Something's very, very wrong here.

As the French citizens had a common name for a common foe, "an enemy of the Republic," so the gay activists have a name they slap on anyone they're at odds with, "the homophobe."

Few modern words have been so inaccurately and unfairly utilized as has the word "homophobia." A phobia is an unreasonable fear or dread of an object, causing a person to avoid the object and provoking a panicked response in its presence. Now, there may be people who are terrified of homosexuals and homosexuality, unable to tolerate its presence, and thrown into panic when confronted by it. But in most cases, the term simply doesn't apply. There are bigots, of course, who unreasonably hate and mistreat gays. The term "prejudice," "bigotry," or "stupidity" might better apply to them. But the misapplication of "homophobia" doesn't stop with them. It is slapped without hesitation on anyone who states that homosexuality is wrong, unnatural, whatever. How convenient to simply dismiss the arguments of anyone who opposes gays by saying, "He's homophobic—end of discussion." And in more and more circles, the label "homophobe" carries a stigma as great as the label "white supremacist" or "neo-Nazi."[11]

So a clever system has been set up here. The homophobe is the enemy that has to be stopped. The homophobe is anyone expressing views on homosexuality contrary to the pro-gay viewpoint, whether his views are founded in religion, personal conviction, or prejudice. The "damage" the homophobe does warrants a removal of his freedom of speech and religion through any means, and, of course, the church is the major promoter of homophobic viewpoints.

In short, the church must either change its views or be silenced.

How can we respond to the militants? First, through repentance. We can, and must, admit our wrongs. Yes, their tactics are deplorable and unwarranted, and no, there's no justification for the terrorism they're inflicting on us. But we have to admit our part, however large or small, in the animosity, and so perhaps we are reaping, in part, the very hatred we've sown.

Second, we cannot allow ourselves to become what they say we already are: hateful, mean-spirited bigots. It would be easy to respond to their hatred with a bit of our own, but—and this is vital—*that's exactly what they want us to do*! It will only validate their accusations against us. Evil cannot be overcome with evil; it can only be overcome with good.

But good doesn't mean weak, which is my third point. We cannot afford to be coerced into silence. The Christian church is perhaps the last organization that continues to promote values which forbid homosexual practices. The militants know that, and that makes us an important target.

In a way, this is a continuation of the controversy of the gospel. Whenever Christianity is preached in its fullness it challenges prevailing viewpoints and inconveniences somebody. Christ Himself is a case in point. He gained popularity through His teachings and miracles, which made Him a distinct threat to the position of power held by the chief priests and Pharisees. They openly admitted that if people continued to follow Him, Rome would sense an insurrection, step in and take over the local government, and thus remove the Pharisees and priests from their position of power (John 11:47,48). Paul found himself in a similar position when he preached in Ephesus. His preaching caused many Ephesians to abandon their idolatry, which put a noticeable damper on the sales of idols and infuriated the local "idol manufacturers" (Acts 19:25-27). In both cases, a concern for the people who might benefit from the gospel had nothing to do with the actions taken against Christ and Paul; rather, these actions were taken because the promotion of Christian belief was undermining the political and social agendas of certain people who demanded that its promoters be silenced.

There is the possibility, then, of nothing less than full-scale terrorism in the near future, terrorism intended to frighten us into either changing our views or never expressing them. If we allow ourselves to be so intimidated, we will deserve the contempt of society, the displeasure of God, and the place of spiritual impotence we will surely find ourselves in.

Who knows? Persecution has traditionally strengthened the church. Perhaps the onslaught of gay militancy will unite us in ways unthinkable until now.[12]

The Church and the Moderate

Not all homosexually oriented adults are radicals. Most, in fact, probably don't approve of radical tactics, although they rarely speak out against them. In my opinion, the majority of homosexually oriented adults are moderates. They live and work among us, make major and significant contributions to our culture, pay their taxes, and want simply to live their lives as they see fit.

There are the people we wouldn't normally envision when we think of "gay." Whether or not they're open about their sexuality, there is nothing in their demeanor or behavior that is offensive. Many of them are likable, responsible citizens.

We seldom identify them because they seldom identify themselves to us. When they do, our response to them should be no different than to any other person: one of respect, consideration, and the normal concern we express for anyone's soul.

Remember, the goal of the church is not to make "straights out of gays." It is to preach the gospel, and there's no reason an exception should be made for the gay moderates. They are not forcing a political agenda on us, as their radical brethren do. So our first priority, as with anyone else, is to share Christ and treat our fellow humans with courtesy and honor.

Often people ask, "How do you witness to a gay?" The question itself shows a certain misunderstanding. Why should witnessing to gays be any different than witnessing to anyone else? Their homosexuality is not our main concern. The state of their souls is. And if the gospel is something they're not interested in, we should respect their free choice as we should anyone else's. We needn't feel obligated to argue over sexual matters with people who have no interest in such an argument. I see no reason why a Christian should automatically target a gay friend or co-worker as an object of reformation. "As much as possible," Paul said, "live at peace with all men." That's a good Scripture to keep in mind when responding to moderates.

Actually, I feel the best way to witness, at times, is to listen. And when witnessing to a gay friend, listening may be your most effective tool. It may also be educational for you.

Glenn Wood refers to a friendship he struck up with a gay university professor. The professor is someone Dr. Wood obviously admires; he describes him as an outstanding teacher and an intelligent, likable individual.

He didn't know the man was gay until they'd had several conversations together. Once he acknowledged his homosexuality, he began telling Dr. Wood what his life was like—how it felt to have watched 32 of his friends die of AIDS, how being a victim of gay bashing had affected him, how cruel he felt some Christians had been to gays in general. Dr. Wood, who apparently did more listening than talking, describes his reaction:

> I had been transformed on that thirty-minute conversation. I had vicariously experienced the pain of another human being... by the grace of God and the openness of a fellow mortal, I gained new insight into the anguish of this world.[13]

The Church and the Fighter

We are all playing Christian club games while men and women around us are tormented by sin, too timid to bare their bosoms, too ashamed to ask our help.

—John White,
Eros Defiled

The church's response to the Fighter largely determines whether or not he'll keep fighting. All the counseling offered to him in this book is still in vain if he doesn't have a church to love him, support him, and relate to him.

So first off, we need to recognize the existence of homosexually oriented believers in our churches. I hope by now you will agree that they exist, and if they exist, a need for ministry exists with them.

There's no reason ministries to such people can't be developed in our churches. After all, when we preach against the evil of a lifestyle or activity, we should also be seeking alternatives to offer in place of the thing we're condemning.

Our response to abortion is a good example of alternative action. For years we've railed against the crime of murdering the unborn, yet to the woman in crisis pregnancy we offered little in the way of alternatives. Naturally, telling people they were doing the wrong thing without helping them do the right thing was unsatisfactory. Finally we realized we had something other than condemnation to offer. Christian ministries to women in crises began to appear. Halfway houses for single mothers gave women a safe place to complete their pregnancies without financial burden. Christian adoption networks took some of the administrative burden off women who opted for adoption instead of abortion. Crisis pregnancy counseling became a common outreach activity of many churches. We had cursed the darkness long enough; it was time to light a candle.

To this day few such candles exist for the Fighter. Yet we can't deny the prevalence of homosexuality and so, as we did with the abortion issue, we've got to establish ministries that will meet the special needs of the Fighter.

Support group ministries are one good alternative. We see such groups in many churches for believers dealing with substance abuse, divorce, relationship difficulties, smoking, and eating disorders. Why is homosexuality, clearly a major problem, so often neglected? Forming a group to address the issue is no major undertaking. I'd like to offer a few ideas on establishing such a group.

Specialized ministry groups should never take the place of church fellowship or a normal social life. They should, rather, supplement it. That should be made clear from the start.

The function of such a group is to provide a safe, godly environment where people can openly discuss their homosexual struggles; learn from the experiences of others who've gone through similar struggles; be accountable to a group of Christians who are genuinely concerned; and know they have friends who are regularly praying for them, available to them, and rooting for them.

Mature leadership is mandatory for a group like this. And the leadership does *not* have to be made up of people who've experienced homosexuality. (That's a common misnomer—only "ex-gays" can minister to gays, only "former drug addicts" can minister to drug addicts, etc.) It would be far better, in fact, if more people who've never been involved with homosexuality would involve themselves in these ministries. All parties could learn from each other, and come to realize how much they really do have in common.

It doesn't take a lot of expertise to develop these ministries. Some basic knowledge about homosexuality is helpful, of course, and groups like Exodus International can provide useful information. But a willingness to be involved in the lives of Fighters is the starting point from which solid, successful ministry to them can develop.

Which brings us to the larger issue of discipleship and intimacy in the church. When we function as a body—a group of believers who acknowledge their need for each other, who take time to know each other, and who commit themselves to each other's welfare—we create a godly environment where healing of all kinds can take place. That is the most effective way to address the needs not only of the Fighter but of all Christians. Solid, bonded relations in the church are a more noble goal than large congregations, fancy programs, and bigger buildings. That is the essence, the form of Christianity that expresses Christ's intention for His people.

> *Love, and the unity it attests to, is the mark Christ gave Christians to wear before the world. Only with this mark may the world know that Christians are indeed Christians and that Jesus was sent by the Father.*
>
> —Francis Schaeffer

Appendix
and
Resources

APPENDIX

Answering the Pro-Gay Theology

If I profess with the loudest voice and clearest exposition every portion of the truth of God except precisely that little point which the world and the devil are at the moment attacking, I am not confessing Christ, however boldly I may be professing Christ. Where the battle rages, there the loyalty of the soldier is proved.

—Martin Luther

As of this writing (July 1991) five major denominations have considered or are considering a revision of their traditional views on homosexuality. The General Assembly of the Presbyterian Church (USA) has overwhelmingly rejected a committee report asking for, among other things, acceptance of premarital sex, homosexual relationships and teenage sexual activity. By a 534 to 31 vote the general assembly said no to all of the above.

It remains to be seen whether the United Church of Christ, the Episcopal Church, the United Methodist Church, and the Evangelical Lutheran Church in America—all of whom are currently involved in similar debates—will follow suit. Much depends on the influence of the more liberal factions in each group, and how much pressure they can apply to their denominations at large.

Although church groups supporting acceptance of homosexuality seem to be in the minority (a telephone poll of 100 adults taken for *Time*/CNN showed that 81 percent of the respondents who frequently attend church feel that sexual contact between men is always wrong),[1] they are a powerful minority indeed to have made such inroads that the subject is even under discussion!

The debate over homosexuality and the Bible—specifically, whether or not the Bible condemns homosexual acts in all cases—will do no less than rip the body of Christ apart within the next decade. It will force believers to declare, in black and white terms, where they stand on issues of sexuality and biblical interpretation. And the emotions generated during the debate will, as always, color and cloud the issue.

You are already participating in the battle. Whether you're a Fighter, a family member impacted by a loved one's homosexuality, or an interested party, at some point you'll be approached by someone who will claim that Scripture doesn't forbid homosexual practices. That person's argument will force you to give an answer for your beliefs, part of which should include a response to what I call the "Pro-Gay Theology."

In essence, Pro-Gay Theology argues that, while the Bible is authoritative, it is either not *fully* authoritative (it is subject to error in certain social issues) or it has been traditionally misintrepreted in the area of homosexuality. It is, as I see it, a system of beliefs based on objections to the traditional viewpoint of Scripture and sexuality.

"Our pews are empty and our outdated attitudes about sex have a great deal to do with it," complains Marvin Ellison, professor of Christian Ethics at Bangor Theological Seminary in Maine.[2] The good professor would have us believe that our attitudes toward sex should reflect those of our culture, that filling pews is more vital than objective truth. Yet Dr. Greg Bahnsen of the Southern California Center for Christian Studies insists that "when the church begins to look and sound like the world, there is no compelling rationale for its continued existence."[3]

The dilemma of homosexuality for many Christians also fuels the objections of many pro-gay advocates. They claim that their attraction to the same sex feels perfectly normal and natural. "If it seems natural," they say, "must it not therefore be God-given?"

While a specific scriptural response to this question is detailed later, a general look at the question and a bit of history will shed some light on the beliefs of the pro-gay apologist.

The advent of the Universal Fellowship of Metropolitan Community Churches (UFMCC), founded in 1968 sparked a new approach to homosexuality and religion. The UFMCC, attended largely but not exclusively by self-identified Gay Christians, claimed there was no conflict between homosexuality and Christianity. The initial precepts that the church (and the budding Gay Christian movement) was founded on were rather general: God loves gays as much as He loves anyone else, the gospel invitation is extended to everyone regardless of orientation, and since gays found little refuge in the Christian church at large, a new fellowship was needed to welcome them and affirm their total personhood, homosexuality included.

They were right in many ways. God indeed loves gays as much as anyone else, the gospel invitation is certainly open to them, and the church's response to them has generally been very poor and often hostile. Their interpretation of Scripture, however, causes many Christians, myself included, to take serious issue with their position. Their testimonies seem to show a pattern of placing personal experience above biblical standards. "If I'm still gay after trying not to be," they seem to say, "then

God must have made me this way and so there must be a better way of looking at the Bible."

What lies behind such cavalier use of the Scriptures? Some would say rebellion, others would say a reprobate mind. I say it's deception.

Deception is an element of the end times which is seldom stressed, usually because turmoil in the Mideast or ecumenical trends steal the spotlight during discussions of Bible prophecy. Yet deception is a recurring theme in both Christ's and Paul's descriptions of the last days.

> The disciples came to Him privately, saying ... "What will be the sign of Your coming and of the end of the age?" And Jesus answered ... "Take heed that no one deceives you" (Matthew 24:3,4).

> Many false prophets will rise up and deceive many (Matthew 24:11).

> So as to deceive, if possible, even the elect (Matthew 24:24).

> God will send them strong delusion, that they should believe a lie (2 Thessalonians 2:11).

> Evil men and imposters will grow worse and worse, deceiving and being deceived (2 Timothy 3:13).

The deception of the end times, which for many reasons I believe we're living in, has an easy target in those of us indoctrinated by the self-love philosophy promoted in the 1970's and solidified recently even in the church. This philosophy expresses itself through a variety of modern heresies, including the "Name it and claim it" teachings, the Positive Confession Movement, and the

Pro-Gay Theology. Particularly vulnerable is the Christian with homosexual desires, who is often seduced into thinking that seemingly natural inclinations are in and of themselves justification for violating biblical standards.

When I was being interviewed by comedienne Joan Rivers on her talk show, this philosophy came through to me with new clarity. Regarding my stance on homosexuality, she asked me, "But if God gave us these feelings, how can it be wrong to express them?" She was sincere. Like many people, she assumed the very presence of a feeling indicates its divine origins. "If it feels good, do it," we used to say. Today's version goes several steps further. "If it feels good, sanctify it!"

Deception usually expresses itself in a challenge to God's Word. "Has God indeed said?" the serpent intoned in Genesis 3. "Does the Bible really say?" the liberal theorist asks. Same song, second verse. And the appeal of deception is usually to the area of life we are the least willing to yield to God's authority.

That, as I see it, is why we are in the midst of this debate. Below I've listed the most common points of pro-gay theology as "Objections," because they represent objections to common views on homosexuality and Christianity. "Responses" are also included. They will, I hope, be of help to you when your biblical position is challenged. As always, you'll need to include your own insights and observations.

General Objections

Objection 1. Jesus said, "Come unto me, *all* ye that are weary and heavy laden," not just "Come unto me, all ye that are heterosexual." The gospel is for everyone, including gays.

Response. True, Christ's invitation is to everyone. Most Christians who believe homosexuality is unnatural do not believe that homosexuals cannot be saved—

only that they, like all of us, are called on to repent of all aspects of life that are contrary to God's standards. (Remember that the first word of Christ's public ministry recorded in Matthew 4:17 is "Repent.") We are *all* called to repent just as surely as we are all called to salvation. Further, to say that no change in behavior or heart is necessary *after* conversion is to deny the very need for conversion in the first place. The Scriptures teach that Christ takes us as we are, then begins to bring all areas of our life, sexuality included, into subjection to Him, as modeled in His conversation with a woman taken in adultery:

> *Jesus said to her, "Neither do I condemn you* [I take you as you are]; *go and sin no more"* [repent] (John 8:11).

Objection 2: If gays didn't ask for their orientation, then God must have created it, so how could He condemn it?

Response. There is nothing in Scripture to suggest that if a thing seems natural it is inevitably God-given. But there is *much* in Scripture which condemns many "natural" states and desires:

> *The natural man does not receive the things of... God* (1 Corinthians 2:14).

> *[You] were [before conversion] by nature the children of wrath* (Ephesians 2:3).

> *The carnal mind is enmity against God, for it is not subject to the law of God, nor indeed can be* (Romans 8:7).

> *Behold, I was brought forth in iniquity* (Psalm 51:5).

The heart is deceitful above all things, and desperately wicked; who can know it? (Jeremiah 17:9).

Objection 3: The church has shown condemnation, not love, to gays.

Response. True, in many respects. The problem here is not the church's *adherence to biblical principles,* but the harsh way that many Christians have promoted those principles ("The Bible condemns homosexual acts, so gays are horrible people") and the church-sanctioned actions that have been taken against homosexuals. This once held true for other areas of behavior as well. For example, in Puritan times if a woman was found to have gossiped, she was tied to a stool, dunked in a lake, and held underwater for as long as a minute. Likewise, if a man neglected his attendance at church, he was put into wooden stocks for public humiliation. The problem was not the fact that the church denounced gossip or lack of fellowship, but the cruel treatment that people guilty of these things received. The answer is a balanced, compassionate method of promoting biblical truth, not a negating of that truth.

Objection 4: People use Bible verses to justify violence against gays, so it's potentially harmful to quote the Bible when criticizing homosexual behavior.

Response. The perverse use of certain Scriptures to justify violence is nothing new, and is remedied by proper use, not banishment, of those Scriptures. We wouldn't consider (I hope) neglecting to teach the Scriptures in which Jesus claims to be the only way to salvation because certain groups have used that claim to persecute people of other faiths! If a tool, like the Bible, is misused, the problem is the *misuse* and not the tool itself.

Objection 5. People are saved on the basis of their faith in Christ, not their sexuality, be it homo or heterosexual.

Response. Affirming heterosexuality as the biblical norm is not an implication that heterosexuality saves people, any more than affirming the biblical injunctions against stealing does not imply that honesty saves people. Salvation through Christ and sexual morality are two distinct issues that should be kept separate.

Objection 6. There are many openly gay Christians who love God, experience spiritual realities, and have specific gifts and callings just like other Christians.

Response. The presence of spiritual gifts, whether preaching, evangelism, or any other gifts, is never an indication that the person in whom those gifts are manifest is justified in all other areas of life. Nor is the presence of God's Spirit in a believer proof that the lifestyle of that believer is pleasing to God. A quick glance at the experience of Christians from New Testament times to the present shows that Christians can be subject to serious error in belief or behavior and still manifest a Christian testimony. The Galatian church had fallen into legalism, the Ephesian church had lost its primary love for Christ, and the Corinthian church had suffered schisms and disorder in its assembly. Yet when these disorders were addressed by Paul and by Christ Himself, there was no implication that these churches were filled with unregenerate people. Just as their error in no way nullified their salvation, so their salvation in no way nullified their error.

Objection 7. Jesus said, "Judge not, lest ye be judged," so when you say that homosexuality is wrong, you're guilty of being judgmental.

Response. Then we had better do away with huge chunks of the Old and New Testaments, because they're both full of statements about right and wrong. Jesus *did* teach that we cannot accurately address someone else's sin without first addressing our own (Matthew 7:1-4). But then He turns right around in Matthew 7:5 and tells us that, having examined ourselves, we *are* to address their sin! Additional commandments that He gave His disciples could hardly be fulfilled without first discerning whether a person's behavior was right or wrong (Luke 9:5; Mark 8:15; Matthew 18:15-19), and statements by other New Testament writers require judgment on our part when dealing with church discipline, doctrinal error, and social contacts (Romans 16:17, 1 Corinthians 5:3-5; Galatians 6:1; Ephesians 5:11; 1 Thessalonians 5:14; 2 Thessalonians 3:11-15; 1 John 4:1).

Objection 8. The Bible teaches us that the main duty of man is to love God first and then to love his neighbor as himself. That's got nothing to do with our sex life.

Response. On the contrary, that has everything to do with our sex life, as it has everything to do with every other part of our life. The command to love God is not fulfilled just by feeling love and reverence for Him, but by expressing our love in very practical ways: "Thou shalt love the Lord thy God with all thy heart, and with all thy soul, and with all thy mind, and with all thy strength" (Mark 12:30 KJV). Body and soul, mind and strength—nothing less. If we are unwilling to conform to God's will in any of these areas, then we have no business saying that we love Him. The question isn't whether or not we *claim* to love God, but whether or not *our actions are in harmony with His expressed will.*

Objection 9. The church used to believe that the Bible justified slavery, subjugation of women, and other heinous practices. If Christians were wrong about those issues, who's to say they aren't also wrong about homosexuality?

Response A. Using that same logic, we'll have to abandon all absolute views on anything for fear of being wrong.

Response B. Those who justified slavery by biblical passages misread the passages, quite likely to suit their own prejudice. Nowhere does the Bible *commend* slavery; rather, it acknowledges its existence. Additionally, not all passages translated "servants" mean literal "slaves," but often mean "house servants" or "employees."

Objection 10. Writers of the Bible knew nothing about loving, committed relationships between homosexuals. All they knew of homosexuality was the kind that was practiced in temple prostitution or idolatrous ceremonies, so of course they condemned it in that context.

Response A. If the Bible was just another book of theories and allegories this argument might stand. But if it is indeed God-inspired, intended as a guide for belief and conduct, then it is unthinkable that God—who is no respecter of persons—would be so careless as to offer no guidance in His revealed Word to the thousands of homosexuals He knew would exist throughout time, if indeed their relationships were legitimate in His sight.

Response B. Even if it could be proven that there was no such thing as a "committed homosexual relationship" in biblical times, biblical authors such as David, Daniel, Ezekiel, and John were prophetically inspired to write about things that were to exist in the future as well as things that did exist at the time of their writings. Surely, if homosexuality was legitimate and natural, there would have been some reference to homosexual relationships in the future, if not the present.

Specific Scriptural Objections

But if I were a Christian homosexual, I think this one question would disturb me most: am I trying to interpret scripture in the light of my proclivity, or should I interpret my proclivity in the light of scripture?

—Paul Mooris,
Shadow of Sodom, 1978

You shall not lie with a male as with a woman. It is an abomination.... If a man lies with a male as he lies with a woman, both of them have committed an abomination (Leviticus 18:22; 20:13).

Objection 1. Prohibitions against homosexuality in the Levitical code have no relevance to us today because Christians are not under the law (Romans 6:14).

Response. The fact that anything is forbidden in Mosiac law (which covers issues as diverse as ceremony, diet, sex, and clothing) does not make for a compelling argument for prohibiting it today if it is forbidden *only* under the law and nowhere else in Scripture. We are indeed under grace and not the law. But it is notable that God's commandments to abstain from homosexual acts are contained in chapters 18 and 20 of Leviticus, which deal primarily with behaviors that are condemned in both the Old and New Testaments (incest, idolatry, homosexuality, adultery, witchcraft).

Objection 2. Jesus said nothing about homosexuality in any of the Gospels. We should base our beliefs on the teachings of Christ, not Paul or the other New Testament writers.

Response A. First, that doesn't mean He said nothing about homosexuals during His earthly ministry—only that we have no record of His doing so. John said that all the books in the world couldn't contain a full account of Christ's works (John 21:25).

Response B. There are several serious offenses Christ doesn't mention in the Gospels—child molestation, rape, spouse abuse—yet we wouldn't assume that any of these were acceptable simply because of their omission from Christ's teaching!

Response C. As important as they are, the teachings of Christ are not the only focus of the Gospels. His life, work, death, and resurrection are also accounted for in these books, with the Acts, Epistles, and Revelation giving more detailed instructions in areas of conduct and belief.

> *For this reason God gave them up to vile passions. For even their women exchanged the natural use for what is against nature. Likewise also the men, leaving the natural use of the woman, burned in their lust for one another, men with men committing what is shameful* (Romans 1:26,27).

Objection 3. The people committing homosexual acts in Romans chapter 1 were idolaters who worshiped images, not God; therefore that passage does not condemn homosexuality, but only idolatry and the subsequent excesses that often go along with it.

Response A. The chapter condemns both idolatry and a variety of practices (not just homosexual) that *sometimes* stem from it, but which are condemned apart from idolatry. For instance, covetousness and fornication, listed in verse 29 of the same passage, may have also stemmed from the reprobate nature of the people described herein, but they are also named as sins in and of themselves throughout Scripture, as is homosexuality, whatever the origins.

Response B. Homosexual desires and actions are described in this passage, independent of idolatry, as being "vile affections," "against nature," and "unseemly," again, *in and of themselves.*

Objection 4. Chapter 1 of Romans does not condemn homosexuality, but homosexual acts committed by people who are really *heterosexual.* They "changed their nature." Since homosexuality was not "natural" to them, they should not have indulged in it, but the passage does not condemn homosexual acts between people who are *genuinely* homosexual.

Response A. Paul's wording here is not nearly that vague. Had he meant to imply that homosexual attractions were unnatural only to *heterosexuals,* he could clearly have said so (as in "the men who were basically *heterosexual* became basically *homosexual,* thus changing their true nature"). Instead Paul uses wording that appears even stronger in the original Greek.

The Greek words he uses for "men" and "women" here are rare in the New Testament, being used only when the writer wishes to emphasize the gender of the subject. When we see the word "man" in the Gospels and Epistles, we are usually seeing a translation of *anthropos* which carries a more general meaning (much the way we use "men" or "fellows" to refer to men in general, and "male" when we want to emphasize gender status). Only when New Testament writers similarly wished to emphasize gender did they resort to the term for man Paul uses here in Romans 1: *arseen,* a word used only here and in Matthew 19:4; Mark 10:6; Luke 2:23; and Galatians 3:28, all of which are Scriptures wanting to emphasize gender to make their point. The same is true of the term he uses here for "women," which is *gune* in lieu of the more common *theleia*, which is usually used to refer to women. *Gune*, like *arseen*, emphasizes the gender of the subject and, like *arseen*, appears in the New Testament only in verses emphasizing "female."

These terms are crucial to the argument. Paul especially emphasizes in Romans 1 that homosexuality is unnatural to the man *as a male* (*arseen*) and to the woman *as a female* (*gune*), not because of what may or may not be natural to their personality, but because of what is unnatural to their *gender*.

Response B. If Paul in this chapter only criticizes homosexual acts committed by people to whom they did not come "naturally," shall we then assume that the rest of the sins listed in Romans 1 also are sins only if they are committed by those to whom they do not come "naturally"?

Response C. These people do not appear to have been heterosexual men and women committing homosexual acts, since Paul describes them as "burning in lust" for each other. "Burning in lust" is an intense phrase which hardly describes predominantly heterosexual people indulging in homosexual acts for convenience's sake (as often occurs in prisons).

Response D. If these people *had* truly been heterosexual and were now truly homosexual, thus changing their nature, the homosexuality itself is still described in clearly derogatory terms, with no clause stating that it would have been normal if they had *always* been homosexual.

Pro-gay apologists are prone to say that, if a person is truly homosexual, he can never become truly heterosexual, yet they often quote this passage as an example of truly *heterosexual* people committing a sin by becoming truly *homosexual*. Are we then to assume that a person who is heterosexual can become homosexual, but a person who is homosexual cannot become heterosexual? Something's wrong here.

Objection 5. The activity described in Romans 1 is excessive, impersonal sex—pure lust without love. That, not homosexuality, is the problem here.

Response A. Romans 1 is not a description of a Roman orgy. Paul in no way indicates that the sexual activity here between men and men or women and women is highly promiscuous. It is *the very nature of the sexual conduct itself* that he considers unnatural.

Response B. When other Scriptures condemn heterosexual lust and indiscriminate heterosexual wantonness, this also provides clear guidelines for heterosexual behavior. No such guidelines exist for homosexual behavior.

> *Do not be deceived. Neither fornicators, nor idolaters, nor adulterers, nor homosexuals, nor sodomites ... will inherit the kingdom of God.*
>
> *Knowing this: that the law is not made for a righteous person, but for the lawless and insubordinate ... for fornicators, for sodomites* (1 Corinthians 6:9; 1 Timothy 1:9,10).

Objection 6. The Greek word *arsenokoites*, commonly translated "abusers of themselves with mankind" or "homosexuals," did not mean that at all, but meant "male prostitute."

Response A. The Greek word *pornos*, used by Paul and translated "fornicator" in the passages above and numerous other places, technically means "male prostitute" and would certainly be used by Paul when referring to one. (Although it is sometimes interchangeable with "fornicator," the meaning is clearly male prostitution, as the word *pornos* is the masculine counterpart to *porne*, which is without exception translated as "harlot" in the New Testament (e.g. Matthew 21:31; Luke 15:30; 1 Corinthians 6:15; Hebrews 11:31; James 2:25).

Response B. Arsenokoite is derived from two Greek words—*arseen*, meaning "male," and *koite*, meaning "couch" or "bed," usually with a sexual connotation, as in Hebrews 13:4: "Marriage is honorable in all, and the bed (*koite*) is undefiled" (KJV). The combination of the two terms does not even suggest prostitution—only sexual contact between two men.

"If people want to accept homosexuality as normal, that is their option, but they do so against the indisputable teaching of the Bible." So say Doctors Glenn Wood and John Dietrich in *The AIDS Epidemic: Balancing Compassion and Justice*.[4] I agree. To disregard traditional teaching is risky—it's even more foolish to disregard the obvious facts: Homosexuality is *never* mentioned in Scripture in anything but negative terms, both Old and New Testament writings contain prohibitions against not only homosexuality but sexual relations of all kinds outside heterosexual marriage, and there is nothing in the entire Bible offering any commendation of or instruction for homosexual relationships. The pro-gay theology is laid on a very shaky foundation indeed.

Resources

J.A. Konrad, *You Don't Have to Be Gay,*
Pacific Publishing House, 1987
P.O. Box 5756-K
Newport Beach, CA 92662-5756

Andy Comiskey, *Pursuing Sexual Wholeness,*
Creation House, 1989

Frank Worthen, *Steps Out of Homosexuality,*
Love in Action
P.O. Box 2655
San Rafael, CA 94912

Elizabeth Moberly, *Homosexuality: A New Christian Ethic,*
Attic Press, 1983

Gerard Van Den Aardweg, *Homosexuality and Hope,*
Servant Books, 1985

Dr. J. Nicolosi, *Reparative Therapy of Male Homosexuality,*
Jason Aaronsen, 1991

AIDS Ministries

Glenn Wood and John Dietrick, *The AIDS Epidemic: Balancing Compassion and Justice,*
Multnomah Press, 1990

Jerry Arterburn, *How Do I Tell My Mother?,*
Oliver Nelson, 1989

Families

Barbara Johnson, *Where Does a Mother Go to Resign?*
Bethany House, 1979

Barbara Johnson, *Fresh Elastic for Stretched Out Moms,*
Fleming Revell, 1986

Barbara Johnson, *Stick a Geranium in Your Hat and Be Happy,*
Word, 1990

John White, *Parents in Pain,*
Word, 1979

George Rekers, *Shaping Your Child's Sexual Identity,*
Baker House, 1982

James Dobson, *Love Must Be Tough,*
Word, 1983

Ministry Referrals

Homosexuality

Exodus International
P.O. Box 2121
San Rafael, CA 94912
(415) 454-1017

Parents and Loved Ones

Spatula Ministries
P.O. Box 444
La Habra, CA 90631

AIDS

Aids Resource Ministries (ARM)
12488 Venice Blvd.
Los Angeles, CA 90631

Notes

Introduction

1. Consider a few statistics from *U.S. News and World Report*, June 10, 1991, vol. 110, no. 22: 1 in 5 Americans loses his or her virginity by age 13; at least one third of married men and women have had an extramarital affair; more than half of all teenage girls are sexually active by age 16; and 6 to 7 percent of the men surveyed were homosexual.
2. The founder and director of Desert Stream Ministries of Santa Monica, CA, and author of *Pursuing Sexual Wholeness*.

Chapter 1—You Are Here

1. Such as the Catholic organization "Courage," "Homosexuals Anonymous" (a Christian 12-step support-group program), and "Transforming Congregations" (a Methodist program).
2. Corrie ten Boom, *The Hiding Place* (New York: Bantam Books, 1971), p. 203.
3. John White, *Eros Defiled* (Downers Grove, IL: InterVarsity Books, 1977), p. 144.
4. Francis Schaeffer, *True Spirituality* (Wheaton, IL: Tyndale House, 1971), p. 26.
5. Ibid., pp. 27-28.
6. Troy Perry, *Don't Be Afraid Anymore* (New York: St. Martins Press, 1990), pp. 339-340.
7. Francis Schaeffer, *The Great Evangelical Disaster* (Westchester, NY: Good News Publishers, 1984), p. 137.

Chapter 4—Laying the Foundations

1. Dave Hunt, *The Seduction of Christianity* (Eugene, OR: Harvest House, 1984), p. 209.

Chapter 5—Why Me?

1. John Money, *Venuses, Penuses, and Sexology* (Buffalo, NY: Prometheus Books, 1986), p. 252.
2. Neurobiologist Simon LeVay of the Salk Institute in San Diego has studied the hypothalamus' of 41 cadavers: 16 heterosexual men, 19 homosexuals, and 6 heterosexual women—and concluded that, because one bundle of neurons in the hypothalamus was nearly three times as large in the heterosexual men as in the homosexual men and heterosexual women, sexual attraction to men or women may be governed by genetics making homosexuality an inborn trait. His report has been met with applause in

some quarters and skepticism in others. ("My freshmen biology students know enough to sink this study," declared Anne Fausto-Sterling, Professor of Medical Science at Brown University in *Time* magazine, September 9, 1991, p. 61.) LeVay himself states his findings do not establish "cause and effect" (*Los Angeles Times*, August 30, 1991, p. A1) although they are significant and should be studied further. They, too, *may* indicate genetic predisposition, although Richard Nakamura of the National Institute of Mental Health sums it up best: "This is a very interesting initial result, but it will require a much larger effort to be convinced that there is a link between this structure and homosexuality (*Los Angeles Times*, August 30, 1991, p. A40).

3. Richard Friedman, *Male Homosexuality* (New Haven, CT: Yale University Press, 1988), p. 71.
4. Ibid., p. 73.
5. W. Fairbain, "A Revised Psychopathology of the Psychoses and Psychoneurosis," from Peter Buckley, ed., *Essential Papers on Object Relations* (New York: New York University Press, 1986), p. 83.

Chapter 6—The Process of Change

1. When the subject of change in sexual orientation is discussed outside of a political agenda, theorists tend to be more open to the notion of choice and change. Examples can be found in Fensterheim and Baer, *Don't Say Yes When You Want to Say No* (New York: Dell Books, 1975), in which the authors encourage dissatisfied homosexuals to resist rather than accept homosexual fantasies (pp. 226-231), or in Masters and Johnson, *Homosexuality in Perspective* (Boston: Little, Brown, and Co., 1979), in which Masters and Johnson ascertain their client's goals—whether or not they're satisfied with their homosexuality—and treat them accordingly. Andrew Morrisin, in *Shame: The Underside of Narcissism* (Hillsdale, NJ: The Analytic Press, 1989), relates a case of a Mr. Dowland who was homosexual, had no desire to change, but began to experience heterosexual attractions during the course of his therapy as a result of other emotional issues being resolved (pp. 93-94). It is impossible to know how all psychologists, psychiatrists, and psychotherapists feel about the possibility of changing sexual orientation, but it seems that many would at least allow anyone the right to try.
2. John Money, *Gay, Straight, and In-Between* (Baltimore: John Hopkins University Press, 1988), p. 117.

3. Glenn Wood and John Dietrich, *The AIDS Epidemic: Balancing Compassion and Justice* (Portland, OR: Multnomah Press, 1990), p. 238.
4. Ruben Fine, *Psychoanalytic Theory, Male and Female Homosexuality: Psychological Approaches* (New York: New York Center for Psychoanalytic Training, 1987).
5. Gerard Van Den Aardweg, *On the Origins and Treatment of Homosexuality* (New York: Praeger Publishers, 1986), p. 197.
6. Irvine Bieber and Toby Bieber, "Male Homosexuality," *Canadian Journal of Psychiatry*, vol. 24, no. 5, 1979, p. 416.
7. Lawrence Hatterer, *Changing Homosexuality in the Male* (New York: McGraw Hill, 1970), p. 138.
8. Patricia Hannigan, president of the Orange County Psychological Association, quoted in the *Los Angeles Times*, interview, April 5, 1990, Life section.
9. Other programs treating homosexuality include Masters and Johnson, who reported successful results (71.6 percent after a six-year follow-up period) for homosexually oriented patients wanting reorientation [*Homosexuality in Perspective* (Boston: Little, Brown, and Co., 1979), p. 402]. Feldmon and MacCulloch reported a 72 percent complete or near complete absence of homosexual fantasies among 25 treated patients, who, after treatment, were either heterosexually active or had heterosexual fantasies [Birk, Miller, and Cohler, "Group Psychotherapy for Homosexual Men," from Clifford J. Sager and Helen Singer Kaplan, eds., *Progress in Group and Family Therapy* (New York: Brunner/Mazel, 1972), p. 681]. Birk, Miller, and Cohler found that, after two years of group therapy, 42 percent of their patients had shifted to or toward heterosexuality. Additionally, 92 percent of the patients claimed their therapy was valuable, and 65 percent said their depression had improved (Birk, Miller, Cohler, *Progress in Group and Family Therapy*, p. 708-709).
10. Kinsey's statistical data is currently under fire through a book by J. Reisman and E. Eichel, *Kinsey, Sex, and Fraud* (Lafayette, LA: Huntington House Publishers, 1991). The authors take serious issue with the population from which Kinsey drew his conclusions about the prevalence of homosexuality.
11. Kinsey, Pomery, and Martin, *Sexual Behavior in the Human Male* (Philadelphia: Saunders Press, 1948), p. 638-641.
12. Ibid., p. 639.

Chapter 7—Maintaining Sexual Integrity

1. "Sexual fantasy ... often depends on a basic judgment made